Being Mrs. Mom

A Christian Woman, Wife, and Mother Living in the 21st Century

By Makeda Rodriguez

Copyright © 2016 by Makeda Rodriguez,
http://beingmrsmom.com

Published by In Faith Books

All rights reserved. No part of this book may be reproduced or utilized in any form or by any means, electronic or utilized in any form or by any means electronic or mechanical, or by any information storage and retrieval system—except for brief quotations for the purpose of review, without written permission from the publisher.

Published & Printed the United States of America

ISBN: 978-0692538807

Cover design: Makeda Rodriguez
Interior design: Makeda Rodriguez
Content editing: Makeda Rodriguez

You are welcome to use a short excerpt of this book for review purposes. For other queries, contact makeda@makedarodriguez.com

Want to more information on Being a Christian Woman, Wife, and Mother/ Being Mrs. Mom visit
http://beingmrsmom.com

Scripture taken from the New King James Version.
Copyright ©1982 by Thomas Nelson, Inc.
Used by permission. All rights reserved.

Dedication

This book is dedicated to my grandmothers, my mother, my aunt, and my daughters for teaching me to laugh and live loved.

To my grandmother Marion because of who you were and still are to me.

To my Nana, Diana, because you are a treasure that I have found to be priceless.
I love you.

Contents

DEDICATION

TELL THEM THAT I LOVE THEM

INTRODUCTION

GETTING FOCUSED

BEING A WOMAN

BEING A WIFE

BEING A MOTHER

SOME OF LIFE'S LESSONS

YOUR RELATIONSHIPS

FINAL THOUGHTS FROM THE AUTHOR

ABOUT THE AUTHOR

Tell them that I love them

Says The Lord

"So many of my people are afraid to be themselves, but I love them just like that.
They confuse My love with the love of people.
People love based on actions. I love regardless of actions.
Even this confuses them because although I love them, I can hate what they do.
Their actions change who they are and their quality of life, making their lives resemble death.
Yet, still...nothing that they do can make me love them anymore or any less."

Introduction

In 2014, after moving back to the east coast, completing my Bachelor's degree, being accepted into my graduate program, celebrating our 12th wedding anniversary, and having our fourth child, my grandmother and great grandmother passed away within two weeks of each other.

These two women, represented to me, a time that I could never get back or truly comprehend. They had displayed a strength and wisdom that had been imparted into me. It required me to live with a certain caliber of integrity, which is now ingrained in my soul.

My paternal grandmother, when she passed, was 75, born in 1939; her mother, my great grandmother, was 93 and born in 1923. Both of them took something with them, their stories.

My maternal great grandmother passed while my family and I were away on military orders in Utah. Her mother before her, passed away when I was 5 years old.

This is why I say that I have been blessed with a treasure, a gem, a diamond in the rough, my Nana. She is the last of my grandmothers that can share her story. She can give me a glimpse of what life was like before me, my daughters, and even my mother.

With this realization, I have determined within myself that it is important to <u>LISTEN</u>…to write, document, and share my story, for I maybe the last one to tell of their stories and to document my time.

This book, I dedicate to grandmothers before me and my daughters who long to hear the impact that life has on other people's stories.

I want to say that I do not think that my story will encompass all that life has to tell nor will I bare all of the details of my life's burdens. However, I have acknowledged the call of God on my life as a writer and answered that call with a yes.

It is my hope that you might be blessed by the words in this book. I pour out my heart, humbly, asking God to grace you as He has graced me with the power to live in our time, as a woman of God…a woman of integrity.

I have written on my blog for the past 10 years and it has been a great desire of mine to pull the words from the virtual world and into reality, where the words can be held in our hands and read on a page.

While I will definitely share content from my blog, within these pages, I have also taken the time to go a little bit deeper, to find the nuggets that have been hidden away for you.

You may find that my story is not unlike your own. I am a woman, struggling with some of the same things that you struggle with. I am a mother, hoping that she is raising her children right. I am a wife, praying that the spirit of divorce would not have a stronghold in my marriage; that my husband and I will continue to grow stronger, together.

I pray, I sing, I cry, and dance. I have fun and I get bored. I am a woman, like you and I can relate to your story.

My prayer for you, as you read this is that God would touch you, as He has me, and empower you on this mission of encouragement. For it is, what I believe, He is calling us to do. He wants us to encourage one another with our stories because within the pages of our stories is His story. Through our lives, He will touch, change, heal, and strengthen many. I pray that you are blessed and strengthened to live out the Word of God; not as a cliché, but as a true disciple of Christ. I pray that you are motivated to be the woman that you will be proud to introduce to your grandchildren; not because of your degrees or your finances, but because of your integrity and your relationship with God.

Let me warn you of this. You will not always agree with what I write, but let it be a catalyst for prayer and seeking of the Lord's will for your life and His opinions. Allow my words to cause you to question yourself, your motives, and your tendencies. For I measure myself with the Word of God and challenge you to do the same.

Be blessed.

Sincerely,

Makeda

Here's to Being Mrs. Mom

How to Read this Book

Some books come together like stories that can be read from cover to cover, weaving the threads between the chapters of characters and events. They send you on highs and lows, causing you to be lost in the author's story.

This is not one of those books.

Within the pages of this book, I share essays, blogs, and thoughts from my heart on being a woman of God who desires to be great for her God in all areas life. Although it can and should be read from cover to cover, the threads that you will find weaving each section and chapter together are the words of God from the Bible.

These scriptures are meant to get you to focus on His perspective for you. Read my thoughts and realize that I am talking to you. I have prayed that you would receive what God has for you through my writings. Understand that this is meant to be a tool of encouragement for you, not just a story.

This is not about me.

It's about you and your journey with God throughout your life, as He has journeyed with me throughout mine. I have just chosen to share with you the ways that life has tried me and God has blessed me.

I don't want you to get lost in my story. Instead, you should be reminded of elements of your own story and how God has nudged you in the past to do, be, and say. As you are reading this, you should feel that you have to stop for a moment to think and ponder.

This book is not conclusive.

There is so much more that God has given me to say, but I don't want to overwhelm you.

Read this and be challenged, be refreshed, be encouraged.

Read the scriptures and highlight the words that stand out to you throughout the book. Write in the margins. Join in the conversation with me. Talk back and pray about the things that I say that challenge you.

Look at my stories and understand that I am a woman, like you and that this life is not always easy, but God makes all things new and beautiful.

That's the essence, the sweet smelling fragrance that should be with you as you read this book. It is the reason for the flowers on the cover.

We each have scars, bruises, and struggles, but as you go throughout this book, see how I have overcome. If I cannot tell you anything else, it is that God is faithful and that I have overcome.

Do you want more?

Well, then…you have to just keep on reading.

the older women likewise, that they be reverent in behavior, not slanderers, not given to much wine, teachers of good things— that they admonish the young women to love their husbands, to love their children, to be discreet, chaste, homemakers, good, obedient to their own husbands, that the word of God may not be blasphemed.

~Titus 2:3-5

My Grandmother Marion

I remember what it felt like when I found out my grandmother, Marion, had passed away. The day prior, I was driving down the street and kept thinking that I needed to call her. I hadn't spoken to her in at least six months. I could give so many reasons as to why. There was the busyness of having four children and moving. At that time, I was dealing with marriage and military life; finishing my degree and being 8 months pregnant; or even being too far away. However, none would be, in retrospect a reason for me not to have talked to her in so long.

Driving down the street thinking this thought, I told myself that I would call her. I made my way to pick up my children from school and commenced with my normal day. The next time that the thought crossed my mind, I told myself that I would call tomorrow.

The next morning, I was up getting my children ready for school. My husband was downstairs and my phone rang. It was my father. He normally did not call me this early, unless it was important.

I could hear him loud and clear as I walked down my hallway toward the stairs. His words pushed through and passed me, causing my legs to buckle. "Grandma Marion has passed." I felt something leave me as I collapsed to my knees and cried...

I had never experienced such a feeling in my life. I have never fainted, got weak in the knees, or lost control of myself, besides experiencing muscle failure in the army, at least that I can recall. For moments on end, which today, still feel like hours, I just sat sobbing.

Why didn't I call her?

It would have been my opportunity to say goodbye...yet, she would have told me to say "see you later."

To this day, at this very moment, I can hear her calling me her angel baby. I can see her beautiful smile and, as the tears stream down my cheeks, I am so thankful for the love and joy that I was able to experience by having her in my life.

Letting go of her will always be one of the hardest things that I ever have to, for she is in me and will always be with me...

My Grandma

I am reminded of your sincere faith, which first lived I your grandmother Lois and in your mother Eunice and, I am persuaded, now lives in you also.
2 Timothy 1:5

Nana

Every day presents new opportunities, new relationships, and new challenges. I have sat for hours on end, contemplating various aspects of life. I have wondered about the events that transpired before me and the experiences of my ancestry. I have watched as women live and I have observed that for many of us, something is missing.

When I was a little girl, I remember my grandmother Diana, whom I call Nana, singing and dancing as she cooked in the kitchen. I remember listening to her play music with smooth tones, depth of the bass, and beats of the drums. I would play with my toys and watch as my mother and grandmother prepared breakfast and enjoying life. My grandmother, my mother, and my aunt, in their best moments would laugh for hours on end. Moments like these stuck with me. If you were to ask my children, they would tell you that I do the same things.

Nana loves spaghetti, rice with okra and tomatoes, and a nice black cherry soda. As many of us have, I too adopted the tastes of my family. My husband says that we eat pasta at least once a week, but I enjoy it as much as my grandmother does. These are just some of the similarities that I have like my grandmother. There are many more in our physical qualities and habitual activities, but as you can see, she has always been an important element of my development.

I remember when I was growing up seeing how she took care of herself. She took great care in how she styled her long natural hair. She applied her make up and left her perfume on the dresser, only for me to follow and observer the beautiful golds, blacks, reds and whites that she had purposely used to decorate various area of her room.

Classic, sophisticated, and eloquent, those are the words that I would use to describe my perspective of Nana, as I was growing up. Knowing her as my elder would deeply impact my attitude toward life, people, and experiences.

When you are a child, you think of childish things. We understand little of what the things we see, ear, and experience really mean. As a child, I never wondered about Nana's life. I never questioned her experiences. I knew that she loved me and would always be there.

I talked to her in my youth and more so in my adulthood, but after the passing of my grandmother Marion, I realized that family is only with us for a season. They mold us and shape us, but there is great value in who they are, the sound of their laughter, eve in their chastising words of wisdom. Nana and I began talking on the phone more and more. Conversations that I had with her at previous times in my life began to make more sense and I began to ask more questions. She told me of her mother, grandmother, and other family members. She explained her life, lessons, and hardships. As I listened, I realized that she was a goldmine of wisdom.

After being on the phone with her for hours, I began to realize that much of who I was today was because of Nana. My entire life, she has been present. Whether in the physical or the spirit, she was always there. She has prayed for me and my household more that I'm sure I can imagine. She has laughed with me, been frustrated with me, seen me at my highs and my lows, yet she has always given me the same guidance, "God will take care of it."

When I asked Nana what she would want young women to know about her, she said that she is a God fearing Christian woman. It was also important to her that we know and understand that she always had the support of her mother and grandmothers as she was growing, maturing, and raising her family. She emphasized to me that our world is different because so many women are alone. No one is saying anything to the women of today. No one is helping them raise their children or learn to love their husbands. No one is showing them that they are valuable, how to love God, and take care of themselves.

Listening to her heart for young women, reminded me of something, my own thoughts. I have felt and thought the same things. I have been concerned for my generation of women and the ones that are coming after us and wondered where the support is. Everyone is so preoccupied with their own lives that they have forgotten about community. If community exists it is either rare or it's not genuine. People are only there to get what they can get. They are not willing to sacrifice themselves for the sake of helping another woman, as she raises her children or prays for her husband. I'm sure that this exists on a small scale, but the vast majority of our society has forgotten about their neighbor.

Nana has given me something that I am eternally grateful for. She is my grandmother, but she is so much more. She is my sister in Christ, prayer partner, confidant, and my friend. I have learned through her that we have ups and downs, but God is always there. She has showed me that we make mistakes, but we have to learn from them. She has showed me how to listen and how to speak; how to love my children beyond themselves and to nurture them past their humanity. She has forgiven and covered sins, been tested and tried, loved, lost, and cried, but most of all she has been faithful to God.

I know that she is not perfect in the natural, but that's the best part about her. She doesn't have to be perfect, she's my Nana and I couldn't ask for anything more. She has showed me that striving to be perfect spiritually is more important than anything. I wish that you knew her, had an opportunity to speak to her, and listen to her because she really is a treasure.

The fear of the Lord is the beginning of wisdom,

And the knowledge of the Holy One is understanding.

~Proverbs 9:10

My Thoughts

Let's take a step backward to when I had first started working on this book.

It was the first month of 2016, but the last month of my 32nd year on this earth. I had chosen to use the month of January as a time to reflect on my life, so far, and to plan for the rest of my life.

Some people had done this in December because it was the close out of the year, but I was still finishing projects, preoccupied with Christmas celebrations, and family activities. I had not truly taken the time that I needed to reflect on all the things that I had endured within the past year, let alone the past 32 years of my life. For that reason, I gave myself the time I believed I needed to rest, reflect, and refocus myself.

Many people, bloggers, readers, family, friends, and were looking for my thoughts. I don't say that to mean that they are eagerly awaiting my words, but instead to say that no one really knew where I was at that time in my life, mentally, spiritually, professionally, and emotionally. I was doing different. I was being quiet.

"For thus the Lord GOD, the Holy One of Israel, has said, "In repentance and rest you will be saved, In quietness and trust is your strength." But you were not willing, (Isaiah 30:15)

There was a time in my life where I had not been the woman I am today. I was outspoken and flamboyant. I thought that my opinions should be heard by those that rejected them the most. I looked to the Lord to make known the truths that He had shown me, but the lack of understanding that radiated from those that surrounded me, left me frustrated. Ultimately, I felt misunderstood.

Those were my younger years. In those times, I wanted the peace and rest that would be found in God, but if I am to be honest, I wasn't willing. I didn't want to wait. I was afraid to trust Him. I thought that He was like the people in my life. I feared being forgotten.

I have found that throughout the duration of my life, I had a tendency to give all of my thoughts, ideas, and jewels away before the set time to release them. Growing and finding myself approaching a new place in my life, my 33rd year, grab hold of my life lessons. I desired to be wiser, more productive, consistent, and diligent. These are all qualities that I have possessed in small amounts, but my desire was to continually live them out fully.

Let's fast forward a bit to the current

As I told you, I started putting this book together in the first month of this year. Now that I am in the last month of 2016, I look back and I am thinking of my journey, my feelings, and my experience. There are things that I want to say to you. I want you to know that this message comes from the bottom of my heart.

I want you to be blessed in all that you do, but that means that you have to live life and give it 100%. You have to be willing to take a chance on your relationships, your dreams, yourself, and mostly on God.

There are a lot of things that will come up against you as you go forward in life. Remember, you are not perfect. Although you are striving to be perfect, as our Father in heaven is perfect, you cannot hold yourself to such high human expectations that you do not allow yourself to make the choices that you will grow from…aka…mistakes. This will sound like a contradiction in a moment, but please know that I am speaking about your own expectations here.

I have been nervous about you reading this book, not because of any of the normal reasons. Instead, I have been nervous because I hope that it embodies all that God has desired for me to put into it. My attention has been given to many things, but in the end, I realized that I was called to do this. My struggles, lessons, and motivations, were all examples of what to and not to do as you are living out your life.

You may be older than I am, younger than I am, or even my age, but please recognize that wisdom does not simply come with age, instead it comes with experience and seeking God. I do not consider myself wise because I have been there and done that. Instead, I believe that God has given me nuggets to share and through Him, I have gained wisdom in my life to live in the fear of the Lord, for this is the beginning of wisdom. This might be my one and only time and opportunity to reach you, so hear my heart for you. I want you to be you. Be determined to allow the essence of what God has put in you to shine through to the world.

Prior to deciding that I would write this book, I had chosen to be silent. As the Lord revealed to me that it was time to put this book together, I began to wonder why I had chosen to be silent. Was it because I wanted to find my strength in the Lord or was it out of fear?

For a while, it was out of fear. I was afraid of what my readers would think. I was afraid that I wouldn't be able to meet the expectation that had been set for me. I was afraid that I would say too much and that I would be left in the same place that I had found myself in years prior, misunderstood. Yet, this time was different.

I was no longer silent because of fear. I was silent because I knew the importance of seeking the Lord. I was tired of trying to figure it all out. I really wanted the Lord to show me what He wanted me to do in my life.

When I stopped doing everything and sought God about my path, everything began to unfold. Today, I am the owner of a business, an author, a coach, and more importantly, I am unapologetically me. I am me because in my silence, I found His strength. The strength of God empowered me to say that which was necessary and needed. I learned how to use my voice and how to walk in my own skin as a woman, wife, and mother.

I had been learning this over time, but in the months prior to writing this book, my silence revealed the truth to me through the magnification & manifestation of God's presence in my life. I had come to realize that God had been changing me and making me better, but due to my own failure to view myself through His eyes, I was not walking in my call as an author.

I realized that although I walked in faith in many different areas, this was the area that lacked action and you know, faith. It's an action word. I had to make a choice. I would no longer find security in, simply, writing the blogs that could be edited and deleted on a whim. I had to do what God had called me to do years ago, write books.

As you read this book, I want you to ask yourself this question. Why are you being silent? The truth is that your silence plays a part in the culture that we live in. A friend of mine has a blog called Fiercely Silent, and I love what she says…

"Fiercely Silent is having the courage to tear down the barriers that have been erected to keep every woman from reaching her God-given destiny. [We are] living Fiercely Silent as we stand as warriors who have risen to the challenge of leading others to freedom. Being brave and courageous is not about being perfect or being visible. It is about being unafraid to be invisible to reach those who are forgotten."
~Natasha Tubbs

Use your voice

There was a time where I had struggled. I really struggled and had been praying and seeking God about the direction that He wanted me to go in.

I have been blessed with talents and abilities. I have been given opportunities and chances to do such wonderful things. Yet it is very important to me that I fulfill my purpose.

A few years ago, I sat down and wrote out my mission statement. However, knowing my mission does not mean that everything will go the way that I think it will go. Over the past few years I have heard God call me to a place where He desires to use me to help others.

I found that, while waiting on Him to work it all out, I was tested and tried by life.

I have fought battles in my mind and thoughts that challenge my existence. They challenged my call. They challenged my abilities, talents, and relationships. I have had to listen to the Holy Spirit within me. He said that I am here for a reason; I am called and chosen; my talents, abilities, and relationships are all purposefully blessed.

In this, I find myself thankful. I might not have it all together. Yes, I am walking it out, but there is one thing that I have learned over the past few years.

I have a voice

God has given me a voice. He has blessed me with a strong one too. So, I choose to use my voice for good. I choose to use my voice to encourage you. I use my voice to bring Him glory.

Today, I want to encourage you to do the same thing. If you feel like you have it together, ask yourself if you are using your talents, abilities, and voice to bless others.

If you are like me and you are watching God put it all together, I challenge you to find your voice and use it to bless someone else. Use your struggles and challenges. Allow them to make you strong. Not just strong enough to recover from the battles that you have fought. Let them make you strong enough to strengthen, encourage, and motivate someone else.

I hope you find this helpful.

As you watch God and use your voice…

"For where two or three are gathered together in My name, I am there in the midst of them."

~Matthew 18:20

Why Should I Read This Book?

You might be asking yourself this question. Think about it for a moment.

We as women, find ourselves at a crossroads in today's society.

Everything that is being shown to us in the media defies who we are and what we are called to do. It challenges our instinct to nurture and encourage because it inspires us to be competitive and on guard against one another. We have lost confidence and trust in building a community of women that will uplift us and hold us accountable because the world has told us that everyone that gives something away always wants something in return.

If you think about it for a moment, you know that women are looking for other women that have things in common. We want women to sit and talk with. We want to have coffee and tea with women who want to strengthen and encourage us.

Many of us don't have anyone to go to, when we have a problem. Music is being played that discourages growth and relationship. Some of the books discourage and boggle us down with untruths.

However, this book is different. Its message is different and I am, well…different. I am your sister in Christ and I know what it's like to feel alone in the midst of a trial. I know what it's like to wish that someone was there when I went through my struggles. God was there and I am very grateful, but even out Heavenly Father said that it's not good for men to be alone, so I craved community.

When you read this book, I want you imagine sitting with me as we talk. I want you to think about having a conversation with a girlfriend that has your best interest at heart because I want you to win.

Realize that God is in charge of our lives.

We grow precept upon precept line upon line and I'm here to encourage you to keep on going.

Create in me a clean heart, O God,

And renew a steadfast spirit within me.

~Psalm 51:10

The Change

I have thought about my life as a woman. I have looked back over my transformation from who I was to who I am today and I have to say that I am thankful for the changes that God has made in me. Yet, I realize that it wouldn't have happened without my willingness to change.

God does not force change on us. Not the internal change. He allows us to decide if we want to be changed or not. When we choose His way, He makes us into something beautiful, but when we don't, we remain in our mess. I am thankful that He didn't leave me where I was.

I have watched, both in social media and in life, as women are making choices that they believe are complementary to their title of "woman of God," but the truth is that they aren't. While some may get frustrated with me for what I am about to say and call me judgmental, I believe that I am just being real…a real Christian woman.

I'm not perfect, but I wish that when I was a young lady, making my mistakes, people didn't just wink at them and say, "Who am I to judge." Instead, I am grateful for the moments when my grandmother, Diana, called me on my mess and told me to stop it.

Those are the moments that I cherish and the times that I am very thankful for. She is the reason why I hold myself to such a high standard. I have read the Bible and I read it every day. I look at what God's word says and I look at my life.

That is the highest standard and since that is my standard, it is the one that I hold you to as well. It's not my own personal expectation, but instead it is the expectation of the Lord.

You may have questions about my life and wonder who I am and where I come from. You will learn more about me as we go on, but it's simple to answer a few questions that will tell you my perspective on it all.

<u>Do you drink?</u> No, but I tried to. I had a hard time with this when I saw in the word that it is not wise for kings to drink strong wine. It said to give strong drink to those that are ready to die and I'm not ready for that.

<u>Do you smoke?</u> No, but I tried to. I had difficulty with this as well, when I realized that the Holy Spirit dwells within me and is grieved when I don't take care of my body.

<u>Do you have sex outside of marriage?</u> No, but I tried that as well and I wish I hadn't. As a married woman, I wish that I had been able to come to my husband pure. I wish that the world made it easier for me to abstain from sexual immorality as a young woman, but as you know, the world is against God and therefore against you and me, if we call ourselves Christian women.

<u>Well, what do you do then?</u> I live my life to the fullest, understanding that I am human and will make mistakes, but once I make them, I learn from them and move forward. I strive to be who God has called me to be as a woman and I turn from all things that He considers evil because I want Him to be pleased with me more than anything else.

<u>How do you deal with sin?</u> Head on and with the word of God.

These topics are all of the things that we hide away as we lower the standard for other people. We lower the standard because we want to tell ourselves that it was ok when we did it, but the truth is that it wasn't ok. God can take any mess that we are in and make it beautiful, but once He calls us on it and reveals to us that it was a mess, we have to admit it. That's the only way that things will get better.

We have to see that we will get nowhere without Him. We have to come to a place where we realize that the things that we call fun, greatly displease the God that we say that we love.

Like you, I have dealt with rejection, depression, rape, and abuse. I have had struggles with my self-worth, finding my place in this life, and understanding my purpose. I have wondered why I went unseen, unheard, unwanted, and denied. I have searched for love in the wrong places, gotten the wrong type of attention, and cried out for help when it seemed like no one heard me. I have cared for those that didn't care for themselves, been told that I was too much, and lost relationships that I greatly cherished. Still, in all of that I have learned that I am who God wants me to be. Not because I remained the same, but because I read His word, prayed, gave myself over to Him, and trusted His process.

Before I did things His way, I did them mine. I did what I had seen. I tried what I had heard. I wanted a life that would be beautiful, but I wasn't sure how to get it. I didn't know that the relationships that I had prior to my marriage would have such a profound effect on it.

You see, this standard that I hold you to, is not because I walk around with my head held high. Nope. It's because I walked around with my head held down for so long. It had a façade of winning, when in fact, I felt like I was losing.

It wasn't until God changed my life at 19, that I began to see things differently.

As the deer pants for the water brooks,

So pants my soul for You, O God.
~Psalm 42:1

Getting Focused

For anything that becomes visible is light. Therefore it says, "Awake, O sleeper, and arise from the dead, and Christ will shine on you." Look carefully then how you walk, not as unwise but as wise, making the best use of the time, because the days are evil.

~Ephesians5:14-16

We have a lot to discuss in this book. We are going to be looking at a few different topics, but before you dive into the pages, I want you to take the next few days to think on the topics that I bring up within the next few pages.

Each day's topic presents a new topic. Each topic asks you a new question. Each question challenges you in a different way.

I understand, you may not feel like doing this, but the reason for it is that we want our time together to be productive. We want the Lord to speak through me to you about the different things that are discussed within this book.

In order for that to happen, I have prayed as I wrote this book and sought God as I put it together. Now you have to think on these things.

After you have read the next seven topics over the course of seven consecutive days, you are ready to dive into the conversation with me about being a Christian woman, wife, and mother.

Day 1

Before we dive into the meat of the book, let's talk about something.

Yes! We all have things to do today. People will tug on us and attempt to pull is in different directions. Our minds will cry out for guidance, but this one thing is true. "God has not given us the spirit of fear, but of power and of love and of a sound mind." 2 Timothy 1:7.

Say this with me. "I have a sound mind."

Say it again. "I have a sound mind."

We must allow the word of God to permeate our being and allow Him to lead us, not the tugging of individuals and systems that need and want us to move as they say.

Yes, obey the authority of the land, meet the deadlines, work hard, be successful, but first…find yourself rooted and grounded in Him.

Take the time before you go, to stop and seek His direction. Give yourself the freedom your soul needs to receive from Him all that you will require for the day.

Take a moment to write down your thoughts and plan for the day ahead of you. If you put Him first, and acknowledge Him in all of your ways, He will make your paths straight and order your steps.

If you think that I'm just talking to you, I'm not. I'm also talking to myself. I have a million and one things that I need to do today, but only God knows what my human capability for accomplishment is on this day and so, with all that I have and all that I am I take the time first to submit myself to Him.

I stop to say, "Father, have your way in my life today. Let Your peace rule and reign in my mind. I will not allow the fear of failure or rejection be the thing that rules my mind. For that is not the type of mind that You have given me. You have given me a sound mind and I have power." Amen

I challenge you to take the same stance that I am taking. Don't be overcome by your to-do list. Start with a clean slate and allow the Lord to help you fill it. He will not fail you. Romans 10:11 says that "no one that puts their faith in God shall ever be ashamed."

I place my faith and trust in Him and I KNOW that HE WILL NOT FAIL ME. I just have to be willing to submit my will to His and follow Him.

You have to know this too!

I pray that you are both blessed and motivated by this today.

Day 2

We go into every endeavor and relationship with an expectation. No matter what we tell ourselves, we are hoping for something. If we were not, we would not move forward into it.

Hope gives us the desire and drive to move forward.

There was a reason why you decided to pick up this book. Perhaps you are one of my blog readers or you know me personally. Maybe you saw the title and thought that there was something within the pages of this book that would do something for you.

Whatever your reason is, it is important that you identify it. Not only do I want you to identify the reason, but I want to take a moment and pray for you regarding this book.

See, Being Mrs. Mom isn't just about me sharing my journey or my story with you. It isn't solely about my ideas and thoughts on life. Instead, it's about encouraging you to a place where you feel confident in who God is in your life and in who He has created you to be so that you are able to walk fully on a daily basis knowing that you loved, wanted, and alive for a purpose.

Maybe you already know this but, you struggle with your intimacy with God.

Perhaps you struggle with your relationships with your family, husband, friends, or children. You could even struggle with your identity, weight, and career. Wherever it is that you find yourself, before we dive into this book, I want you to focus on understanding your personal struggle for a moment.

It is important that you are aware of your current situation. It is important that you are able to say and write down what it is that you are dealing with at this point in your life.

Take out your notebook and write it down. What is it that you are struggling with at this point in your life? What are you expecting to get out of this book? What do you want God to help you with?

Now...

Father, I pray that you help my sister to identify her struggles, so that she can bring them to you for healing.

Day 3

When you picked up this book and chose to read it, you did something. You spoke with your actions about who you are. You said that you are a woman of God.

Do you realize that you do this all of the time, in everything that you do?

When you make daily choices, you are either proclaiming that God is the Lord of your life or that someone else is.

See, I have come to realize that there is a characteristic that defines a woman of God and differentiates her from the other women of the world. That quality is selflessness.

She is selfless because she does not choose to focus on her own desires, wants, needs, and perspectives, but instead she focuses on that of the Lord. She looks to making Christ's name known instead of her own. She desires for God's purpose to be fulfilled in the earth, instead of her own.

Although life is hard and she must work, she is not blinded by her own pain and suffering. No! A woman of God, sees that no matter what is going on, God can get the glory out of the situation, if she submits herself to His will.

She realizes that her prayers are not in vain. Her petitions are not in vain. She understands that every time that she submits a care to the Lord, He hears her. She knows that her family is blessed by her hard times on her knees, crying and weeping. She is sure that although it is rough, her suffering is for a purpose. She identifies the unseen entities that come up against her relationships, her finances, her call and calls on the Lord to intercept the plans of the wicked one.

If you are reading this, it is because you either consider yourself to be a woman of God or you long to be one and are trying to figure it all out.

Let me tell you…this is where you start. You begin submitting yourself to the Lord, knowing that you can trust Him. You bring yourself to a place where you love what He loves and you hate what He hates. You love Him more that all else, including yourself.

What stops you from being selfless? How has the enemy tempted you to let go of what God has given you because you could not see that it would work out well? Have you ever lost your hope? What is your hope in, honestly?

Day 4

Have you ever looked at a strong woman of God and desired to emulate her? Have you ever said to yourself, "I wish I was more like _____?" I know that you have. I think we all have had moments when we think that if we were more like someone else, we would be strong enough, wise enough, or talented enough. We tell ourselves that we are not blessed the way that she is because something about us is defective and just not enough.

I have been at this place before. Earlier in you young adult life, I aspired to be like some of the powerful Christian women that I was watching. I watched how they ministered in humility and strength. I listened to their stories and felt empowered by God through them. I longed to have what they had. I thought that if I could just get what they had, I would be enough and life would look and feel different. I wouldn't have to try so hard because I could have it. So, I strived to be more like them.

What I didn't realize what that these women did not wake up the way that I saw them. They were not born with humility or the strength to empower others. The word of God did not come out of their mouths at their natural birth. Nope, it didn't happen that way.

As I grew and was changed by God, I began to realize that their strength and wisdom had been birth out of their spiritual connection with God as they endured life's experiences. Their strength came from knowing, though experience that God was faithful.

One powerful woman lost an eye. Another endured a childhood full of abuse. One woman that I knew personally was lost her mother and was raised by an alcoholic father that left her emotionally scarred for life.

Yet, they all overcame their adversity by the grace of God and lived to spread His glory. Their strength was birth out of overcoming the pain through the word & power of God.

I have had women put me in this same category of women. They look to me and say, "I wish I was strong like you, Makeda. But, I'm just not strong enough."

With this, I have to humbly say back "What has made me strong enough? What makes me any different from you?"

I have spent long nights crying, calling out to the Lord for strength to keep going. I have told Him that I didn't have the strength to keep being married because I didn't know how. I dealt with rejection from my youth and fear of what people would see. I wondered why I was always misunderstood. I never thought that I was strong enough.

Until God showed me how to be…

He took all of my painful experiences and turned them in to lessons that I could teach my daughters and other women. He allows all of my tears to become prayers that could and would save lives. He showed me that not one whisper of prayer in faith to Him was in vain because He was listening.

You may not understand this right now or maybe you do, but I want to tell you something. I no longer wish that I was those other women, nor do I regret my past. I don't wish that I did not have the experiences that I had or the long sleepless nights. If I did not have them, I would not be able to tell someone to do anything different. I wouldn't have the wisdom that I cried and longed for. I would not be able to help anyone because I would still be a foolish youth, rejected, and longing to be someone else that I'm not.

You are reading this and there is a purpose in it. You have to fully accept who you are in Christ. You have to see that there is a reason for who God has called you to be and for experience that you have had. You have to understand that your failures are not failures, they are learning lessons. You have to know that although you don't understand everything, God does.

I can't tell you why things happen this way, but great things are birth out of suffering, when we seek to live life God's way.

I would not be who I am today, had I not suffered and endured the pain. I would not have known what it means to be humble, had I not dealt with pride. I would not value having a good marriage to my husband had I not first struggled to be a married wife.

My parenting would not be what it is today had I not learned patience in the midst of my frustration. Organization would not be so important to me, had I not first been a chaotic mess.

I laugh at this now, but it is the truth.

The Bible says that it is good for a man to carry his burden in his youth. It also says that we should not despise the chastisement of the Lord, for those whom he loves, he chastises. These two things go together.

God desires to prune us and allow us the opportunity to carry the burden while we are young, so that our elder years can be spent in wisdom. Fools walk in darkness and never look to the light for direction.

If you have desired to be a certain type of woman, but have struggles to see how it can happen, you must look at yourself and pray that God would help you see what needs to be changed. I do not deem that anyone should suffer horrific abuse for the sake of becoming wise. Instead I am saying that when you suffer, it is not in vain.

You don't have to remain in abusive relationships. You don't have to minimize your value. However, pray that God would help you to have the right perspective.

Day 5

How many times have we said it? "I just don't have enough faith."

Many of us have found ourselves where we are looking at our level of faith and thinking that it isn't enough to get us past a certain place in our lives.

I want to challenge you to think of this in a different way.

The Bible says that Faith is the substance of things hoped for, the evidence of things not seen. It says that should seek to please God and that those who desire this must have faith in God. We must believe that He is and that He is a rewarder of those who diligently seek Him. It says that He will do what He says that He will do because He is not a man that He would lie.

If you read the paragraph above, then you realize that faith has little to do with us and a lot to do with God.

When I hear women say that they don't have enough faith, I don't question their faith. I simply question their relationship with God. I wonder do they really know Him. See, when we know Him, we understand that He cannot fail or lie. He is 100% trustworthy and faithful. He does not forget and seeks our good will more than we do. He will not quit or give up. He is always watching and listening. He is always there.

When we say that we lack faith, we are really saying that our relationship with God is strained because we no longer trust Him.

Stop for a second and ask yourself if this is true.

When you are afraid, don't you worry?

When you worry, aren't you concerned?

When you are concerned, do you feel that you have to do something?

These emotions are all brought on by anxiety because you are not trusting God. You believe that He has not heard you, forgotten about you, and could care less about what is happening in your life. You wonder if you are a mere speck in the dust to Him and become frustrated with your situation because you believe that He is not looking out for you.

The truth is that you have forgotten who He is. You have failed to remember His character and to speak to Him about the things that are troubling you. Don't you realize that He is always with you? Do you realize that these feelings of having a lack of faith stem from not trusting God?

Beth Moore talks about this in one of her books, "Believing God." You cannot say that you know Him and attempt to stand upon His promises, if you have not spent time getting to know Him and learning who He is. You have to know that He cannot fail, forget, quit, or give up on you. He is ever working to make things work out for you beyond what you are or were ever expecting.

So when asked, "How can I strengthen my faith?" My answer is simply. You have to strengthen your relationship with God.

As you do that, you will build your faith. Study the scriptures, not for the sake of memorizing them, but for the sake of getting to know the Father, to attempt to understand His ways, and develop a lifestyle that encourages your relationship with Him to grow.

If you do this, life's circumstances will not always make sense, but you will know that He has it all taken care of and that something good has to come out of it.

Day 6

I have had this conversation for a few months, now I want to have it with you.

We are women of God, longing for more of Him. We want more of His time, His guidance, and His grace. We long for all of these things, but they are found in relationship with Him, not in church or in the meaningless things of this world.

We have to stop and spend time with Him.

Have you found yourself struggling with hearing His voice, knowing His will, or just feeling close to Him?

The world tells you to find spend some time in yoga and you will feel better. I challenge this because yoga is a form of worship to another god.

The church and many of the books being published are telling you to spend time, every morning for just 5 minutes doing devotional.

Devotion…that's a good word for time with God. Yet, I believe that it's not used correctly in our society.

See, it's not about spending 5 minutes a day, reading one page in a book, or praying for an hour. It's not about the measure of your time, completing an activity, so that you can feel better and check a box.

It's not about how long you go, but how deep you dive into your relationship with God.

The word devotion means love, loyalty, or enthusiasm for a person, activity, or a cause.

It's a word that explains our reason for the time. It's a word that tells how we feel when we are in communion with God, meeting with Him daily to discuss His heart and our hearts. It's when we lay down our cares at His feet, tell Him our concerns and seek answers.

When you take this word that describes a feeling and turn it into a verb that must be backed by activity.

Devotion changes from a feeling for and turns into a place where you go before the Lord to listen. It becomes what you do.

And yes, I said listen.

We spend so much time listening to so many different things.

How often do you go before the Lord, ask Him a question, and wait for the answer?

I have heard women say that they cannot hear from God and they wish that they could. They say that they pray all of the time, begging Him for answers, but He never answers.

How would you feel if your husband, child, or relative walked in to the room and began telling you all of the things that they wanted or needed? This person asked you a few different questions, took a breath, and then walked away. Would you wonder if they really wanted to listen or if they just wanted to speak? If you had your back turned when they were leaving and were giving the answer, just as they turned the corner, this person could and probably would say that they felt like you weren't listening. They'd probably say that you never answered the question.

Yet, that is not true.

Now imagine God. Every time we draw near to Him, He draws near to us, whether we sense His presence or not. We begin to tell Him about our concerns and go down the list of complaints, petitions, and grievances. Then right when He begins to speak to us, answering our questions, we get up.

I used to do this all of the time. When I was a young lady, I would pray and seek God, but wonder why I couldn't hear Him. Part of my problem was that I wasn't sure how to still myself in order to hear Him.

Then, as I read His word, I heard His voice. I began to recognize a still small voice answering my questions as I prayed. It wasn't audible, but I could hear Him.

I would turn off the radio and journal out my prayers. I would write out my concerns and be honest with Him about my desires. I would sit and talk with Him, as I would a friend about life's concerns. Then I would just listen. I would look out the window, calm myself, and wait until I knew what He was speaking to my heart.

There were times when the answers came by searching the Bible diligently, for hours on end. Then there were times when the answer would come as I washed dishes and prayed quietly for direction.

My life became devotion as I sought God.

I can help you find direction, by leading you to God, but once you are with Him, you must be with Him. You have to stop thinking about God as a thing. You have to stop seeing your time with Him as a duty and mundane. You have to begin to cherish the relationship with Him and realize that He is real and He cares for you.

When you set an appointment to have lunch with a friend, you expect her to show up, right?! What do you do when you sit down to talk with God? Do you look for Him to show up? Do you expect Him to grace you with His presence?

If the answer is no, the you know why you can't hear Him. You aren't listening. You aren't listening because you don't believe that He's saying anything to you, but He is.

I want to encourage you today to do something. Commit to changing your perspective about God. When you sit to talk with Him, before you begin speaking, actually draw near to Him. I personally close my eyes and imagine His presence coming in the room with me.

Pray with expectancy and listen with intense attention to detail. Recognize your idols and distractions. Remove them from your life and turn down the noise.

If you want more of God, you have to remove the things that take you away from Him.

Build your relationship with Him because this is true intimacy.

Day 7

> *"When God created us, He had two purposes in mind. These are demonstrated vividly in the story of the woman at the well. This Samaritan woman was looking for her purpose in all the wrong places: five husbands and one sugar daddy. (She must have been desperate!) Jesus clarified His purpose for her. He told her His intention was to give her life meaning and substance by offering her living water for her soul, so she would never have to thirst again."*
>
> *-Thelma Wells*

READ JOHN 4:1-26 (BELOW)

Therefore, when the Lord knew that the Pharisees had heard that Jesus made and baptized more disciples than John (though Jesus Himself did not baptize, but His disciples), He left Judea and departed again to Galilee. But He needed to go through Samaria.

So He came to a city of Samaria which is called Sychar, near the plot of ground that Jacob gave to his son Joseph. Now Jacob's well was there. Jesus therefore, being wearied from His journey, sat thus by the well. It was about the sixth hour.

A woman of Samaria came to draw water. Jesus said to her, "Give Me a drink." For His disciples had gone away into the city to buy food. Then the woman of Samaria said to Him, "How is it that You, being a Jew, ask a drink from me, a Samaritan woman?" For Jews have no dealings with Samaritans. Jesus answered and said to her, "If you knew the gift of God, and who it is who says to you, 'Give Me a drink,' you would have asked Him, and He would have given you living water."

The woman said to Him, "Sir, You have nothing to draw with, and the well is deep. Where then do You get that living water? Are You greater than our father Jacob, who gave us the well, and drank from it himself, as well as his sons and his livestock?" Jesus answered and said to her, "Whoever drinks of this water will thirst again, but whoever drinks of the water that I shall give him will never thirst. But the water that I shall give him will become in him a fountain of water springing up into everlasting life."

The woman said to Him, "Sir, give me this water, that I may not thirst, nor come here to draw." Jesus said to her, "Go, call your husband, and come here." The woman answered and said, "I have no husband." Jesus said to her, "You have well said, 'I have no husband,' for you have had five husbands, and the one whom you now have is not your husband; in that you spoke truly."

The woman said to Him, "Sir, I perceive that You are a prophet. Jews say that in Jerusalem is the place where one ought to worship." Our fathers worshiped on this mountain, and you Jews say that in Jerusalem is the place where one out to worship." Jesus said to her, "Woman, believe Me, the hour is coming when you will neither on this mountain, nor in Jerusalem, worship the Father. But the hour is coming, and now is, when the true worshipers will worship the Father in spirit and truth; for the Father is seeking such to worship Him. God is Spirit, and those who worship Him must worship in spirit and truth."

You worship what you do not know; we know what we worship, for salvation is of the Jews. The woman said to Him,

"I know that Messiah is coming" (who is called Christ).
"When He comes, He will tell us all things."
Jesus said to her, "I who speak to you am He."

What will you give me?

Many of us struggle everyday with the same questions as the Samaritan woman.

We say things like, "this can't be true! How can anyone love me and provide for me? There must be something that I have to do that makes this possible. There must be a catch. Sure I've heard it before, but it isn't meant to be taken literally."

The truth of the matter is that God already did everything to prove His commitment and love to us, in Jesus.

Now what is left for us is to accept Him and make a conscious decision to love Him and to get to know Him.

Through this, He gives life and life more abundantly. He gives peace like a river, and joy that overflows.

The Bible contains so many promises of God, but few of us every take the time to read them. Unfortunately, when we do see them, we have a tendency to think "that's not for me." Yet that is not what God says.

These things are for those who believe. Do you believe with your heart, mind, soul, and your life?

Do you believe and are you willing to seek Him with your whole heart? If so, let's start.

Being a Woman

*"She openeth her mouth with wisdom;
and in her tongue is the law of kindness."*

PROVERBS 31:26

Woman...

Woman of Faith...

What does it mean to you?

What do those words say to you, when you read them?

Do they provide a window into the life that you have lived upon this earth?

Women of Faith...

Would you attach some other adjective before or after those words that would give a stranger a better understanding of who you are?

These are questions that I want you to ponder and answer for yourself.

Today, women of the 21st century have been given one of the biggest challenges of all time. How will we define our womanhood?

Will we define it by God's definition and by who we are or will we allow the world, a world that cannot identify with our womanhood, to define it? How will we carry ourselves and what will we teach our upcoming generations about women?

There are so many different topics out there that bring about strong emotions in women across the globe. These are issues that cause us to smile, cry…cringe in our sleep. Issues that we pray for and about, but do we realize that God has called us to be women for such a time as this? He has called us to be women of today; women who uphold a standard. Women of Faith…

I think that it is time that we begin to identify what it means to be a woman, a woman of faith.

As of yet, I provide no answers to the questions that I have asked, on this page. I believe that these are topics that the Lord desires for all of us to pray and ponder over. How will we answer these questions?

What do we believe to be fundamentally true about being a woman, a woman of faith?

I will be discussing some of these questions, but it is important that you not wait for me to provide my answer. You and I face the same challenge. Whatever age bracket you fall in, you and I together are shaping history for the women of tomorrow. What will they see when they look back on us? What will they say? How will the women that we are today, encourage them to live tomorrow?

And Adam said:

"This is now bone of my bones
And flesh of my flesh;
She shall be called Woman,
Because she was taken out of Man."

Genesis 2:23

What it Means to Be a Woman

Today, we live in the 21st century, a time that has attempted to redefine everything that is normal, right, true, and good. While there are some things that remain, like the definition of the words like *and, if, but, to*, and *go*, other simpler terms that have never been challenged, as they have in this time have been socially redefined. Yet, I challenge you to consider that the words that we use, whether defined by society or made up by individuals, do not change God's definition of the words.

For instance, women across the world, for generations on end have been the only individuals to have breast and to bear children. Yet, today we have individuals that have created and established methods of defying the natural processes that God has established and turned men into images of women.

Whether these men realize it or not, they have turned the image of a woman into an idol. They have become so enthralled with the image of a woman to the point that they desire to be women. This is something that is key to where we are going with what it means to be a woman because if we can clearly understand that the image of a woman is being idolized we can also begin to understand why it is also being changed and understand why you and I are dealing with such great challenges, in this time that we live in.

When people worship a god, they love it. They work hard for it. They become so passionately infatuated with the thought of this god that they desire the most intimate level of connection possible…becoming one with the god. Now in order to become one with anything, you must adopt its habits, features, tendencies, and character. This is what we do, or are supposed to do when we worship God.

When God created Adam, He said that He made man in His image and likeness. The word that was used in the Hebrew, was the word *tselem*. While many understand this word to be an image, the Hebrews understood the word to mean idol. Now this word, idol meant something a bit different than our word idol means today, at least in this usage.

When the people of the world want to worship, they would create an idol to represent the god that they were worshipping. This idol, was not the god in itself, but instead a representation of the god in the earth. All people that encountered the image knew that it represented the unseen deity that the people were worshipping. It directed the people to worship. Unfortunately, people would worship false gods, instead of the one and true God, but they still had a desire to worship.

Well, when God had created man, in the earth, He desired to make a clear representation of Himself, thus, He created man in His image and likeness. He made an image, a *tselem*, or an idol. Now, remember, this did not mean that God worshipped man, but instead it meant that God wanted all that were to encounter man to understand that man had been given the authority and positioning of ruler over the earth, by God.

Because of the clear representation, animals, the earth, and spiritual beings recognized the authority that man possessed due his likeness of the Father. The sheer viewing of man's countenance would direct all of creation to worship God.

Fast forward to our day and age, men that have lost all respect for themselves and the stature of a man, now desire to become that which they love, a woman. They want to look like, smell like, feel like, and be a woman. They have manipulated their bodies and gone through extreme amounts of agony to emulate that which they worship.

There are two problems that occur when humans create an idol. One is that they directly disobey the Lord and the other is that what they create is never a true representation of the thing. Instead it is a representation of what man desires for it to be. Hence, when we look at the images of women that are being produced by the culture, we recognize that they no longer carry a resemblance to what had been ordained, in character or image.

Women change their eyes, nails, and hair to match that which seems more appealing in the world. They starve themselves or put on extra weight to become "more attractive." There have been cases where women have bleached their skin and gone thru extreme tanning, enduring radiation, to manipulate the color of their skin, which comes from God.

But when we stop to think about all of this, what does it really mean to be a woman?

Adam defined this in Genesis. Woman comes out of man. She is flesh of his flesh and bone of his bone. She is the mother of nations, carrier of generations. She is the mother, the help-meet, and the one that births creation out of the pain, which comes from her womb.

Women are the ones that weep and wail. They recognize the needs of the men and the children. Women are the sisters, the aunts, the cousins, the friends that see beyond the superficial layers of individuals and into their souls to nurture their inner needs.

Women are the resemblance of the Holy Spirt and the Church. Women are naturally lovers, which is why it is so hard for us to understand a man's definition of respect.

Our bodies were created were formed to be vessels of honor that house new life and provide to our husbands what no one else can, intimacy in oneness.

Can you feel it? Can you see it? The world is challenging this definition of who you are. The world calls you the Queen without a King, the Provider, the Boss, the Go Getter.

It tells you that you don't need a man and can do without children. It shouts at you saying "you need no one and nothing." It inspires you to chase after your dreams instead of praying for an understanding of God's dream for you. It shows you that having money and telling all those that hurt you that you don't need them means that you are to rise to the top, while you leave your natural calling behind.

Forget about being a wife and a mother. Never mind, your need to nurture, comfort, and cover the sins in prayer. Ignore that and find your desire to conquer…that is what drives you.

This is what the world says about you. It tells you that your rape, molestation, your silence, and your screaming are all irrelevant. I want to tell you that they are not irrelevant. They are an attempt by the enemy to destroy you so that the life that you were created to breathe in the people that you touch, would never make it to them.

This is not what it means to be a woman.

Do you know?

Do you have any idea, what God says it means to be a woman?

If you found out, would it matter? Would you be willing to shed yourself of the world's identification clothing to put on His covering?

This is my prayer for you. I pray that God would reveal to you, who you are as a woman with all of the standards of the world removed. I pray that He would expose you to the unfailing truth of His word that allows you to trust Him, as you become who He has created you to be. I pray that He helps you to see how He will choose to use your educations, understandings, courage, pains, strengths, and knowledge in ways that will uplift the world, your world in a way that only a woman can. I pray that you would shed your standards that have been based in this worldly society and submit them to the thoughts, plans, and purposes of the Lord.

I ask You Lord, that you would take my dear sister, right now, right where she is and pour out Your love upon her. Help her to see that she is not far from You, but that you want so much more for her. Show her that you do not want her to live in fear of being unwanted, unloved, rejected, forgotten. Instead you want her to live in the being and in the knowledge and understanding that You love her beyond what she could ever possibly imaging. Overwhelm her with your love and show her that you think about her daily, moment by moment; that not a second goes by that you are not wanting her to draw near to You. Help her to see that her weight is not an issue, her finances are not an issue, her hair and her skin are not an issue, but her heart is. Call her back to you and strengthen her as a woman, your daughter...Help her to fight as only she can in a world that has forgotten what it means to be a woman, as a daughter of Sarah.

In the mighty name of Jesus. Amen

*God is faithful, by whom you were called
into the fellowship of His Son, Jesus Christ
our Lord.*

~1Corinthians 1:9

The Trustworthiness of God

Today, I want to invite you to take a look at Psalm 115 with me. Within it, we will find something that cannot be overlooked, the difference between who God is and who the idols are.

Believe it or not, people still worship idols today. To some degree, we also have to be careful of the image that we have of God; for if it is not the correct image, we too are creating an idol. We must know who we worship and serve. We must remember what He is like. We must remind ourselves of His characteristics and when we are unsure, we must go back to the word of God.

When we have the right image of God, we will also recognize that we can trust Him. We will give Him the glory that is due to Him and we will see Him at work in our lives; not because He has finally begun to work, but because our eyes are open to the works of His hands.

> Psalm 115
> *Not unto us, O Lord, not unto us, but to Your name give glory, because of Your mercy, because or Your truth.*
> *Why should the Gentiles say, "So where is their God?"*
> *But our God is in heaven; He does whatever He pleases.*
> *Their idols are silver and gold, the work men's hands.*
> *They have mouths, but they do not speak; eyes they have, but they do not see;*
> *They have ears, but they do not hear; noses they have, but they do not smell;*

They have hands, but they do not handle; Feet they have, but they do not walk; Nor do they mutter through their throat. Those who make them are like them; So is everyone who trusts in them.
O Israel, trust in the Lord; He is their help and their shield.
O house of Aaron, trust in the Lord; He is their help and their shield.
You who fear the Lord, trust in the Lord; He is their help and their shield.
The Lord has been mindful of us; He will bless us; He will bless the house of Israel; He will bless the house of Aaron.
He will bless those who fear the Lord, both small and great.
May the Lord give you increase more and more, you and your children.
May you be blessed by the Lord, Who made heaven and earth.
The heaven, even the heavens are the Lord's; but the earth He has given to the children of men.
The dead do not praise the Lord, nor any who go down into silence.
But we will bless the Lord from this time forth and forevermore.
Praise the Lord!

Having the correct image of God and knowing His character, helps us to trust in Him. If you think about it, this is how we build trust with everyone. Their past actions and understanding their character allow us to feel safe when we are around them. If we know that someone can be relied upon, we know that they will do what they say that they are going to do. When we know that a friend will not share a secret, we feel that we are able to reveal more to them.

It is the same way with God. When we see Him provide for us and protect us on a daily basis, we will trust Him as a Provider and a Protector. However, I also want to mention this.

When we don't take the time to look at what God has done, it becomes easier to forget. When we have experienced hardship in our lives or heard of those that have, it becomes harder to trust God; not because He is less trustworthy, but because we do not see Him in relation to our circumstance correctly.

This is why it is important for us to take the time, every day, to look into the word of God. When we do, we receive a correct image of God, ourselves, and the world around us.

Our God is trustworthy!

The Lord has been mindful of us; He will bless us ~Psalm 115:12

He is not an idol, made by man. He hears our prayers and speaks to our hearts. He reaches out to us and works on our behalf. He dances over us with singing. (Zephaniah 3:17) He is so much more than idol. He is active. He is God.

Every morning when we wake up, it is the Lord that has given us another opportunity to live. It is the Lord that has breathed breath into our lungs. It is the Lord.

Looking at the world and our lives with this sense of His continual working for and doing, to bless us, changes how we view everything. It also changes how we see Him. It allows us to see that He has always been faithful and will continue to be faithful. Having this view, changes us. We come to see ourselves as loved and cared for.

Today I would like to challenge you to take the time to look at your life. What has God done for you? I want you to think about the simple things and the complex. What do you have that you take for granted? Who has God blessed you with? Count your blessings today and look to the One that has made it all possible. Realize that He is working to protect us, even as we sleep. He is always mindful of us. (Psalm 115:12)

Let's attribute this to His character. He is trustworthy. He can be trusted with all that we have and all that we are.

Unless Your law had been my delight,

I would then have perished in my afflicton.

~Psalm 119:92

Watch

"Watch your thoughts;

They become words

Watch your words

They become actions

Watch your actions

They become habits

Watch your habits

They become your character

Watch your character

They become your destiny

~Unknown

The Wondering Mind

Sometimes the mind can get so busy that it just wonders.

Once it starts, there really is no stopping it...

All of the what ifs and how comes that we have been holding back begin to come to the surface of the mind.

There is so much time spent in contemplating the mundane.

There is so much time spent is relishing the things of very little worth.

How does one redeem the time of loathing thoughts and emotions that cause fear and doubt?

The mind...if one can picture it, can be a place of great trial or great travail.

As I sit and think of all the things I could be thinking about, I am thankful that I have a Savior that cares for me...

I am thankful that I don't have to continually think on things that aren't worth my time...

I am thankful that I can focus my mind on positive and uplifting things...

Today, I am thankful that I really don't have what the old folks call... a wondering mind...I just wonder sometimes.

The young lions lack and suffer hunger;

But those who seek the Lord shall not lack any good thing.

~Psalm 34:10

Day by Day

Dear Father
In Heaven, up above
You who poured on me
A great measure of Love
When You sent down
Your Son, Jesus Christ
I was given abundant life,
But I ask You
About the reason You want me to live
I live my life for you
There is nothing that I wouldn't give
You have great plans for me
To prosper me and give me hope
Yet the truth of the matter
Is there are some things
I just don't know
I mean…
Which way do you want me to turn?
How many mistakes will I make?
Before I learn
Will my dreams continue to reach?
The ceiling and then the floor
But deep down inside
I keep yearning for more
More of …
You
What is it that you would have me to do?
I'll keep asking you
I'll continue to see your face
I will take this journey
Of Mine…
With You…
Day By Day

Immediately the father of the child cried out and said with tears, "Lord, I believe; help my unbelief!"

~Mark 9:24

10 Scriptures to Read When Experiencing Doubt

We all have faith issues sometimes. While our ultimate issues of faith are about our relationship with God, we have to also realize what happens in us when we experience doubt. We have to renew our minds with the word of God to combat the doubt. Let's take a look.

Faith vs. Doubt
Faith deals with what you can't see, while doubt deals with what you can.
It sounds confusing, but **Faith** tells you that something that hasn't happened or that can't be seen, will be.
Doubt says that because of what you see or because of what has already happened, things won't be.

Faith As A Gift
It has been said that faith is a gift from God and there is no way to increase it. While I agree with the first part of this statement, the second part is not true.
So then, faith comes by hearing, and hearing by the word of God. ~Romans 10:17
So what does this mean?

Can Faith Grow?
Well, we have all been given a certain measure of faith by God (Romans 12:3), but our faith can grow. (Luke 17:21, Mark 4:24) However that growing is not in the sense of more or less. Instead it is in the sense of being of quality.
The question is not, "How much faith do I have?" as much as it is, "Is my faith strong?"

Without strong faith, doubt creeps in and exposes us to troubles and fears in our lives.

Steps To Take

There are steps that can be taken to help with this process. We have to hear, read, or speak the word of God because these actions produce a hearing in our minds that are needed for faith to come.

So when dealing with ***doubt*** of any sort, it is good for us to have the tools ready and available to usher in ***faith***.

Remember...

- **Hear** the Word
- **Read** the Word
- **Speak** the Word

<u>10 Scriptures to use...</u>

Here are the 10 scriptures to use in these times of doubt.

1. **No Shame-** *For the Scripture says, "Whoever believes on Him will not be put to shame."* <u>Romans 10:11</u>
2. **You Are Loved-** *See, I have inscribed you on the psalms of My hands...* <u>Isaiah 49:17</u>, *But the very hairs of your head are all numbered.* <u>Matthew 10:30</u>
3. **Delivered From All Fear-** *I sought the Lord, and He heard me, and delivered me from all my fears.* <u>Psalm 34:4</u>
4. **Drawing Near-** *Draw near to God and he will draw near to you,...* <u>James 4:8</u>
5. **He Hears You-** *I cried unto the Lord with my voice, and He heard me from His holy hill. Selah* <u>Psalm 3:4</u>
6. **He Is With You-** *Have I not commanded you? Be strong and of good courage; do not be afraid, nor*

be dismayed, for the Lord your God is with you wherever you go. Joshua 1:9
7. **He Cares For You-** *...casting all your cares upon Him, for He cares for you.* 1 Peter 5:7
8. **Peace & Safety-** *I will both lie down in peace, and sleep; For You alone, O Lord, make me dwell in safety.* Psalm 4:8
9. **He Gives Wisdom-** *If any of you lacks wisdom, let him ask of God, who gives to all liberally and without reproach, and it will be given to him.* James 1: 5
10. **He Protects Those Who Love Him-** *Because he has set his love upon Me, therefore I will deliver him; I will set him on high, because he has known My name.* Psalm 91:14

After reading these Scriptures, you should not only find that your faith is a bit stronger, but you should also find that you have more confidence in who God is and how much He cares for you.

Read these Scriptures daily...

Think about them...

Say them out loud...

This is how you will overcome doubt with your faith.

Before I formed you in the womb I knew you;

Before you were born I sanctified you;

I ordained you a prophet to the nations.

~Jeremiah 1:5

Dealing with Rejection

I want to share something with you.

We have all struggled before with being unwanted, unloved, forgotten, uninvited, rejected, and lonely.

The pain of these moments and feelings cause us to bury specific thoughts about ourselves deep within.

Ultimately, we hold on to and carry around the message, from these feelings, of I am unworthy and unlovable.

No one could ever say that they have not wrestled with these things. For they come at us at times when we least expect it, by those that we did not expect it from.

However, if we would take a moment to surrender and trust God, we would hear Him say, as our hearts struggle with all of this pain… "I will never let you go." And if we can believe as our hearts long to, that He means every word of it, we could begin to walk free.

Free from our pain.

Free from our pasts.

Free from the rejection and fear.
We could live as we truly are, not trying to be perfect in the human way of perfection, so that we may be accepted. Instead just being ourselves.

Today, I challenge you, as I have, to look up.

Stop what you are doing.

Find a window, step outside…do something that would allow you to take a look up at the sky, that you cannot touch. The one that proclaims, with its very existence, the reality of God's presence, and hear the Lord say

"I will never let you go. I knew you before you were born. I've known you every moment of your life. I still know you now. I love you. I will always love you. I will hold you with my arms and never let you go."

Then take a breath and realize that you mean more to Him than you could ever imagine.

*Do not be afraid of their faces,
For I am with you to deliver you," says the Lord.
~Jeremiah 1:8*

My Thoughts on Rejection

I want to take a moment to sit down and write about this topic before I lose my nerve, which I already feel is leaving me. There are things that we will all have to endure in this life and rejection will be one of them. I have spent a lot of my years dealing with and avoiding this topic. Today, I have decided to write down a few of my observations and thoughts on the subject.

Today I had an experience in my household that led me to think about this topic. My husband and I had an argument, as real life couples do. Afterwards, we were texting each other about our concerns, when I realized that a few years ago I would have taken many of the things that he said to heart. Today, I was not shaken or moved by his words. I realized that there comes a time in our lives where those that we love the most will reject us. It may not be an extreme level of rejection, but still is rejection.

I wondered what it must have been like for Nana to go through her 72 years of life. How many times had she dealt with rejection from her family, her friends, her husband, her children? How many times had she been faced with the opportunity to be offended? Did she find that she had to grow from the experiences? How did she do that?

Rejection is normally a thing that can rip the heart of an individual to shreds. It can leave someone feeling completely unloved and unwanted. However, when viewed through the correct lens, it leads the believer to realize that God is the only One that will never reject us, as long as we have repented of our sins. He calls us to Himself and made a way for us to be approved.

When the rest of the word is saying no, God is saying yes. These thoughts today brought me to a few conclusions. The first is that some trials strengthen us, others show us our weaknesses. Then there are the tests and trials that reveal to us that we are approved and loved by God.

The other day I was led to read 2 Timothy 2:15. It says *"Study to show yourself approved of God, a worker that need not be ashamed."* Some versions say that we should be <u>diligent</u>. Normally when I would read this, I would look at the diligent part of the scripture. I would focus on studying and completely miss another portion of the scripture. I would work hard and be diligent, as much as possible, to show myself approved of men. I would wonder why my work and efforts were not receiving the approval rating that I had worked so hard to receive. I even wondered what I had to do to get to where I needed and so badly desired to be, in the graces of men.

What I realized was that I never met the standard. No matter how hard I tried, my diligence in private never showed in public. The people that I wanted to see and approve of me, never did. Yet, in the stillness of my life, I could hear and feel the Lord saying that I was enough. He was pleased with me. He had even told me that He was proud of me. But, if I am to be honest, it was never enough.

I kept searching and trying, harder and harder. I wanted people to approve of me. I no longer wanted to be looked at with the eye of rejection because to me it conveyed that I was displeasing. I longed to please. The more I tried, the harder it was.

Now let me be clear. I can say these things in hindsight, but when I was going through these very trying times of my life, I did not recognize it for what it was. I did not know that I was always trying to escape rejection. I did not know that I was trying to people please. I just thought that I was trying my best to be my best. The question was, for whom was I trying? Who was going to tell me that I had done well and it matter enough for me to stop trying? No one would or could say the things that wanted to hear to erase the years of subtle rejection that had added up to a big whole in my heart.

They could never erase the years of pain that I had experienced from my childhood. Raised as an only child, by my single mother, I wondered why I was not enough for my father to stay with me. He was raising my little brother and sister. Later on in life, he had even adopted children. I don't even think that I realized my feelings until later, but they were there. I was too busy trying to cover up and smile to recognize and acknowledge the fact that I was feeling rejected. I wondered why some children had both of their parents, but I did not. I thought that there was something wrong with me that made me unlovable by both parents. And no matter how much time I spent with my father, it never filled the gap that was missing by him not being in my home.

My mother had her own struggles. While I hope to be able to convey the struggle that I faced within my heart, it is still hard for me to do so because she is my mother and she raised me. There is a part of me that protects her because she was, for the longest time, the only one on this earth that gave her time and affections to me. No matter how distorted her version of love was at times, it was all that I had on a regular basis. Now yes, I have to admit that there was a lot of love coming from my grandmothers, my aunts, my father, and my uncles…even my grandfather. Yet the truth remains that the 24/7 giving came from my mother.

If I am to be completely honest, I even felt at times that I was unwanted by her as well. I was a mistake that had happened. Many people had told her to abort me. I wasn't supposed to be here, according to them, but she kept me. She pushed through high school and went to college, but did not graduate until I was an adult. I carried this burden within myself for a long time. I was a burden that she carried which prohibited her from certain pleasures and dreams that she had. I was the reason why she struggled. This is how I saw it. She worked hard to make sure that I had it all. She never told me these things, but remember, I struggled with rejection and I never really felt wanted.

That's what rejection does.

I have worked very hard as a mother to make sure that my children knew that they are very important to me. I want them to know and remember that I have always wanted them. I have stayed at home because I never wanted anything else to compete for the attention of my children or my husband. There are always little things, but I didn't want my job or profession to be something that caused my children to feel unloved.

Today we live in a society that pushes women to be it all and do it all. I had to give this idea up. I am enough. I don't think I can say that too many times. I am enough. I don't need to do more or be more in order for someone to accept and love me. If God, with all of His infinite wisdom and ability, sent His son Jesus Christ to die for me, I am enough. He did that, so that I would know, before I had even had an opportunity to ask for Him to accept me, that I was accepted and loved.

These words seem kind of cliché because people had out John 3:16 a lot. Sometimes, we need to apply it to a specific situation in order for it to have relevance to us. Yes, God loved the world, but He also loved me. That's why He gave His son, for me to know that He accepted me. He knew the challenges that I would face and that I would need Him. The only way that I would even be able to be accepted, after the whole world had sinned was for our holy God to atone our sins for us.

This love is beyond me. Yet, it is the reason why I am stronger today. I am no longer given over to the concerns and harsh words of men on this earth. By men, I do mean people. Their words do not faze me. Yes, I do have my moments, but those words and actions no longer permeate my being.

I realize that my mother and father did their best to love me. They gave me what they had to give. The same is true for my husband. Yet, the truth is that all of this has made me better, wiser, stronger. I know that there isn't anything wrong with me. I'm not perfect, but when I am rejected by people, it doesn't need to stick with me for the rest of my life. It is an occasion that happened.

It is also important to mention that I realized that a rejected thought does not always equal a total rejection of who I am. Disagreement or opposition to opinions should be taken as such, not as a total rejection of me as a human.

The other thing that was revealed to me was the when someone does not like you; it is not your problem. It's theirs. People are going to have issues with us. We have to be in a continual state of prayer. I pray this often. *Lord, create in me a clean heart and renew a right spirit in me.* Knowing that God is always working in me causes me to understand that someone's issues with me don't have to become my problem. That is something that they must work out.

God corrects me when I am wrong and touches my heart when the things that someone else sees are true. Still there is a scripture in the Bible that says *when our hearts condemn us,*

God is greater than our hearts. We need to be willing to change, but it should not be because someone else does not like who we are or what we do. Those are not reasons for change. There has to be some validity to the request for change.

Enlarge the place of your tent,

And let them stretch out the curtains of your dwellings;

Do not spare;

Lengthen your cords,

And strengthen your stakes

Isaiah 54:2

In Times of Stretching

Today I told myself that I would write about disappointments. I wanted to talk how I handle them and my perspective regarding the situations that I face. I mean, who doesn't face disappointing situations…

Yet, I am not exactly sure how this will come together because I am no longer just writing about disappointments, but I am also writing about being overwhelmed and our perspective of God in the midst of it.

These times are what I call **"The Times Of Stretching."**

I just read a post and an email about the emotions and thoughts that we all experience sometimes. The authors posed a question. "Does God put more on us that we can bear?

Who hasn't felt overwhelmed and discouraged…worried or depressed?

I want to say that I believe that we have all felt this way before. I believe that in the midst of a situation or trial, the weight of a thing can feel so heavy that we don't think that we can carry it. Yet, just because we feel a certain way doesn't mean that it is that way.

What do I mean? Trust me, I understand that it may sound like I'm speaking gibberish, but follow me for a minute…

When we are going through any type of trial or testing, we are very uncomfortable.

It's like having a baby…there is pain, but we are able to bear it and for those of us that don't believe that we are strong enough to bear the pain in the end, there is a medication to help up get through it…

Life is this way as well. In the midst of a trial or a situation, we can feel like the situation will never end. Or when it finally does, we will be dead somewhere because we weren't strong enough to make it through.

The thing is…God doesn't expect us to do any of this without Him. He knew what we would endure and what we are made of. He placed certain things in us that only come out when we are tested and tried by fire.

Have you ever thought of the process that a beautiful piece of jewelry goes through before the beauty is revealed?

Beneath the surface of these rocks is something very beautiful, but the beauty is not exposed by gently holding the rock in your hand. People search for rocks that have golden nuggets within them. Yes, they are of high value, but one of the reasons why is because of the unexpected beauty found inside of a thing that seemed to be dead and useless. Have you ever felt that way? I have…

After being tried by the fire and put through a process, something beautiful appears. We are no different…situation, circumstances, and trials… they make us stronger. The trial brings about perseverance. The perseverance brings about character

...for we know that they help us develop endurance. And endurance develops strength of character, and character strengthens our confident hope of salvation. And this hope will not lead to disappointment. ~Romans 5:3-5

Now the question still stands. Does God put more on us than we can bear? No, he does not. He has already given us all that we need to endure the situation. There are qualities in us and the power of the Holy Spirit, coupled together to strengthen us. Are we willing to go through the trial or tribulation?

No trial has overtaken you that is not faced by others. And God is faithful: He will not let you be tried beyond what you are able to bear, but with the trial will also provide a way out so that you may be able to endure it. ~1 Corinthians 10:13

Although a way of escape has been made, we still have to choose to take it. You know, most of the time the test, trial, and tribulation has more to do with the Word and power of God in us, than they have to do with us. We receive the benefits of bearing, overcoming, and enduring a trial, but the trial was there to test the Word in us...

(I digress...)

What happens if we don't choose to take the way of escape that has been provided for us at the appropriate time? Well, we have now taken more upon ourselves than we can bear. God was standing in front of us with a huge sign saying "Take the exit on the right." Yet we chose to continue to veer to the left. This is where we begin to blame God for our short comings, over plate filling, and disappointments.

I do not say this as someone who has not experienced this...Trust me! I know this from experience.

It is imperative that we pay attention and get off at the correct exit. But when we don't, we begin to experience doubt, condemnation, discouragement, and disappointment. We forget that God always has our best interest at heart and we begin to blame Him for our wrong turn. Did you know that sin is to simply miss the mark?

We have all done that and I dare to say that we do it daily…that's why we have and need a Savior.

(Again I digress)

So what are we supposed to do when we have digressed from the path and veered off just a tad bit? It is at this point that we may begin to feel a bit of anger or discouragement within ourselves. Here's what I've learned from my experience and how I've learned to handle it.

- Allow yourself to feel the way that you feel…briefly (DON'T STAY THERE)
- Assess the situation…thoroughly (Ask questions like… Why? Did I contribute to it? Can I do anything better next time? How can I move on?
- Pray for wisdom.
- Accept your part
- Ask God to forgive you & Forgive yourself and others
- Make a list of the things you can do to move forward (pray when you are worried, afraid, tempted, troubled, hurting, angry, bitter, etc.)
- Change your mind about it. (You have power over your own mind and you have the ability to change it. Search the word for what God says about the situation and conform your thoughts to that…this requires believing the word, HONESTLY)

- Remember God can and will work it out for your good.
- Commit to your plan
- Remember that Romans 10:11 says that no one that puts their trust and faith in Him will ever be put to shame.
- Do what you can
- Let God do the rest

These times aren't always easy. In fact, they are some of the hardest times in our lives. Yet, looking back on them, we will see it differently than we feel it now. The goal is to trust God through the stretching, remember that He is on your side, so be resilient.

Yet to all who did receive him, to those who believed in his name, he gave the right to become children of God—

~John 1:12

Why Do We Struggle with Identity?

As women living in today's society, it so hard to identify ourselves and I can personally say that I have been through this. Often times, life wants and tries to identify me by what I'm currently doing, how many children I have, my work status, and even my husband. While all of these are a part of who I am, they are not my identity.

If this is true, why do we struggle with it and how can we overcome it?

Studies have shown that women are relational by nature. We want to connect, deeply, with others. Yet, we generally fear that we are too much for those around us and once those in relationship with us realize it, they will run away in fear, leaving us relation-less.

Due to this relational nature and our desire, we tend to dive completely, heart first, in to our relationships and endeavors. By doing this, we find that we care deeply for the people that we care for. We find that we want to nurture and help them to be the best that is humanly possible. We take the opportunity, while in relationships with others, to cultivate our love and compassion for them throughout our relationship. We want them to know how important they are. In essence, when women love, we love hard.

These loving relationships, if we are not careful, can begin to completely consume us. And this total immersion into the who and what, that we are into, begins to become how we identify ourselves. We become proud of our connections and work.

Remember, when we love we love hard. Do you know anyone that, when they truly love a person or thing, hides it? No, you don't because it doesn't happen that way. Love proclaims, I love _____. So what is the problem with this?

Well the problem is that things and people change. They were never meant to be the indenting factors in our lives. We were never intended to mimic or display the characteristics of a person or a thing; not our husbands or our children; not our jobs or our passions. No matter how great they are.

When I was first married, I had completely lost my identity. I, like many other women, love my husband passionately and this caused me to immerse myself in who he is. However, this total consumption of him, continually, caused me to forget who I was.

While as a wife, I was called to take on my husband's name and cling to him, I was never called to become him. Together we become one, but this is through a process of continually becoming the unified couple that God has joined together in Him.

Not becoming him.

Identifying myself by my husband left me lost, hurting, and confused; it also brought problems into our relationship. I had to begin to learn who I was again and what it meant to be me. Thankfully I had help with this.

Yet, my help was not one that many would think of. It came from God.

Because of how lost, broken, and confused I was, I began to cry out to God for help and He led me to His Word.
Through it, I began to see that I could be passionately in love with my husband and still be me. The me that God created me to be, not the me that I was trying to be for my husband.

I began to learn that God had created me a certain way and this complimented my husband, children, relationships, career, and so much more. I began to understand that my identity in Him was more important than any other identity that I would ever attempt to take on.

Today, my husband says that one of the reasons why our marriage works is because he is he and I am me. However, the struggle to get here was…well hard.

Now how did I get from that point to where I am now?

It was not easy. I had to begin to let the Word of God consume me. Some people thought that I was changing, but if I am to be completely honest, I was. I was changing from the rejected, fearful, and confused little girl who the world and situations had created, into a confident, loved, and courageous woman who God has always known that I was.

I did this one day at a time…one page at a time…one prayer at time.
It's like the Bible says in Isaiah 28:10,

…precept upon precept,
line upon line,
here a little there a little

Yet, at that time, I was in such a hurry. I thought that if I did not hurry up, I would never become…me. The truth is that God loves me so much that He was going to make sure that I was completely identified by Him. His plan was never to leave me the way that I was, so I had to learn to trust Him. The process has been difficult and I continually find that life attempts to define me, but I trust in Him.

The situation for you is that same. He loves you too. If you have read my blog for some time, you know that I have a few favorite scriptures. One of them is 1 Peter 5:7

casting all your care upon Him, because He cares for you.

This has always reminded me that no matter how unloved I feel, I am loved. No matter how much I want to hold on to the situation and take care of it myself, there is a Great and Mighty God that wants to do it more and He does it a lot better than I ever could.

Today I want to encourage you to take that first step in solving the issue of displaced identity. Read Psalm 139 and see what the Lord says about you. Think about how it makes you feel when you realize how much He loves you. Do you see how He sees you? How can it change how you see yourself?

Take a moment, a piece of paper, and pen. Write out your thoughts. This is how your process with begin. By looking at God and becoming aware of your own feelings & emotions.

Remember, you are loved.

Keep your heart with all diligence,

For out of it spring the issues of life.

~Proverbs 4:23

When It's Easier to Pretend

There is a saying that goes something like this, "when life hands you lemons, you make lemonade..." Have you ever heard of it? I'm sure that you have. It sounds like a great saying, but have you ever wondered what is going on between the receiving of the lemons and the making of the lemonade?

Well I have.

I have wondered what the person is thinking and feeling. I have also wondered when it becomes clear that it is time to make some lemonade.

While dealing with these thoughts, it may be hard to focus on the good, to wait for things to get better, or to even know how to feel. At times like this, I think it might seem easier to pretend.

Upset and frustrated, I have often looked at a situation without knowing what to do or how I was supposed to feel. Naturally, I am an optimist. Still there are times when I cannot see the bright side and I feel lost. It is at these times that I start to wonder if it would just be easier to pretend that I am not going through anything at all.

Have you ever felt like that?

Pretending means that you get to ignore the situation. You don't have to talk about it, think about it, or acknowledge anything is happening at all. However, this does not magically stop us from feeling the stress and emotions of the situation. In fact, I think it would make it worse.

By pretending, we would be telling ourselves that the situation did not occur the way that it did. We would also be denying ourselves the right to feel the way we do about what occurred. Denying ourselves of our emotions is not wise because acknowledging our feelings allows us to process situations.

Processing the situations stimulates growth in our lives. There have been many times when I have wanted to stop thinking about a situation. I have wished that it never happened. I have also tried to ignore my feelings about it all. The result is…well ugly.

When I have tried this in the past, I have become very nonchalant and emotionless about various aspects of my life. It is as if ignoring the situation allowed a totally different process to start in my life…I became cold and despondent.

Generally, that is not me. I care, I feel, I wonder. Yet, ignoring situations and my feelings about situations change me. When I allow myself to see the situation, no matter how painful, I feel the emotions attached to it; when I feel those emotions, I process them. In processing them, I begin to learn from the situation. Learning from situations offers wisdom and helps me to trust in God.

I used to ask why God would allow me to go through somethings. I could not see with my eyes, why He would, in all of His infinite wisdom, allow me to endure such situations. It wasn't until I read Romans 5:3-5

"And not only that, but we also glory in tribulations, knowing that tribulation produces perseverance; and

perseverance, character; and character, hope. Now hope does not disappoint, because the love of God has been poured out in our hearts by the Holy Spirit who was given to us."

I realized that the tribulations, no matter how big or small, make me better. They encourage me to a place of being better and hoping in God more.

Now do you see why it is never good to pretend? We don't have to treat others badly and act in a way that is unbecoming, but we should recognize the tribulation and allow the process of feeling, becoming, and overcoming to take place in our lives.

Today, I want to encourage you, as I have been encouraged myself. We have been given some lemons and it's time to make some lemonade.

Sometimes, you may not know how to feel, what to think, or how to act, but continue to trust God. He knew what would happen and He has something great prepared for you in the end. Recognize how the tribulation produces perseverance in you. Take note of how the perseverance produces character in you. Understand how the character produces hope in you. When it is all said and done, look back and see how you are better and the hope that you have in God has not failed you. Remember that it never will.

I hope you have found this helpful and that you will remember these things.
When life gives you lemons, make some lemonade…

Until next time…don't pretend and be blessed.

In God, whose word I praise, in the Lord, whose word I praise, in God I trust; I shall not be afraid. What can man do to me?
Psalm 56:10, 11

A Matter of the Heart, Hurt

In all of my years upon this earth, I have come to learn a few things on matters of the heart. Today I am going to discuss hurt.

It may seem like a very broad topic, but hurt, when it comes to matters of the heart is like a double-sided coin. You just can't win.

If you have been living for longer than 5 years upon this earth, which I suspect that you have, if you are reading this, you have either hurt someone else or have been hurt by someone.

Life is a mixture of sunshine and rain, tear drops and laughter, pleasure and pain. Just remember, there was never a cloud that the sun couldn't shine through. ~Unknown

I set this quote here because I am going to talk about this topic of hurt and it is no easy feat. However, I think it is important to remember that it won't last forever, no matter which side of the equation you are on.

Alright…now let's get into it. When it comes to this heart thing it is either hurt or be hurt…wait! Let me explain. I am not saying this as a thing that should be done; you either hurt someone else or you get hurt. Nor am I saying that you have to make a choice, right now, about which person you should be.

No!

I am saying this as an observation; I want you to think on this, as I explain. Throughout the duration of having a personal relationship with anyone upon this earth, there will come a time where either you or the other person will become offended. This is inevitable. Even Jesus said that it would happen. *"It is impossible that no offenses should come, but woe to him through whom they do come!" Luke 17:1*

Did you catch that? He said that it is impossible that no offenses should come, so the first position that I would like to deal with is the one whom the offense has come to.

The One Who is Hurt

Hurt…hurt comes. It comes in different fashions and forms. It can look many different ways and be very unexpected. There are even times when you can see it coming and attempt to protect yourself, but somehow, it still makes its way to your heart.

If you have ever been hurt, you know that there is a blow to the heart that reminds you that you are more that flesh and bone. I say this because it is not a physical pain that we feel when we are hurt, but instead it is one that goes beyond the physical realm and hits our emotions.

When you are hurt, you can feel like you have done something wrong; you could feel rejected, confused, and even angered by the pain that someone else has caused you. Yet, in the midst of all that you are experiencing you have a choice to make.

What are you going to do?

Various choices can begin to come to your mind. While some options may involve retaliation, I urge you not to make those choices. Yes, I understand that there is only so much that a heart can take and you may feel that you have taken enough, but let me tell you, there is nothing that you will ever do that will not produce some sort of fruit, whether good or bad, that you will not have to eat some day. You will reap what you sow.

Do you want the fruit of hurting another in retaliation? Hopefully you answered wisely and said no.

So what is it that you are supposed to do? Nothing? Now I am not suggesting that you do nothing. Instead I am suggesting that you not be quick to anger or quick to act; don't be quick to speak either, for that matter. (Ecclesiastics 7:9; James 1:19)

Take a moment, whether in a heated discussion or in the privacy of your own thoughts, to take wise Counsel with God. He is near to you, if you draw near to Him, in any moment that you desire and He will give you wisdom on how to act. (James 4:8; James 1:5)

Once you have taken a moment, realize that your actions are very important from here on out. We teach people how to treat us, by how we allow them to treat us and by how we treat others.

If a person has hurt you, it is imperative that you first realize the importance of setting some boundaries. What has this person said or done, or the lack there of, that has caused you to be hurt.

STOP!!! YOU ARE NOT MAKING YOURSELF PROMISES AT THIS POINT!
Don't say things like "I will never allow you to hurt me in that way again." Making yourself promises is not what I am

encouraging you to do. What I am encouraging you to do is to set up some boundaries.

See it
Let's pause for a moment to get a visual...

Two neighbors live with open fields. They are friends and they often travel to one another's houses for fun, festivities, and personal conversation. Crossing the property line has never been a problem. However, both of these families have dogs. When the families cross the property line the dogs have gone with them, in the past. Yet on occasion, when their friends are not going to one another's houses, the dogs cross the boundary line anyway. One family has a garden in the back yard. The other family has a family play set and activities set up in their back yard. When the neighbor's dog crosses the property line, it often leaves its mark. It goes to the bathroom, rummages through the garden, or bites & scratches up the family play set. Both families have noticed the problem.

Without allowing the emotions of being upset to get to them, they simply decide that there is a need for a fence to be placed between the two homes. The dogs have no ill intent, they are just being dogs. Yet there is a need to set a boundary for the dogs, so that each yard can remain as the families would like it to. Each family takes the necessary steps to set this up as they, each, see necessary. Once the fence is set up, the dogs remain where the owners have left them, the yards remain intact, and the families continue to grow in their relationship together.

Getting an understanding
Did you get the visual? I hope so...Did you get what you need to do? I hope so...

You need to decide what the fence is that will allow you to keep your property intact. Now, fences are not walls. They are fences that simply say to other people, this is my property and I would like you to respect my property line. Your dogs are not allowed to go rummaging in my yard; nor can they tear up my family play set.

This is not an easy task, but it is one that needs to be done in order for you to remain unoffended. The offenses will come, but you have to decide how to handle them.

Making the right choice
There will be many options for you, but I suggest that you take time for yourself, so that you can get a grip of how you are feeling and seek God, to know what you need to do.

Just don't make any rash decisions. Choose not to accept the offense as it is, but instead to reevaluate why you are hurt and how you cannot be offended. There will be times when you can see why you are hurt, but cannot see how it is that you cannot be offended. When this happens, you have another option, just forgive. If you have to, forgive yourself for anything that your feel responsible for. Then forgive the person, so that you can move on.

Forgiving does not mean forgetting. Nor does not forgetting mean always rehashing the painful events. Instead it means that you learn from the experience and see how things can work out better next time.

Side Note: Sometimes God allows us to see the character of people. When you see it, pray, and act in a way that honors God, is wise, and is confirmed in your conscience. Pray for the other person because hurt people hurt people.

It is my prayer for you that in the midst of all that you are feeling and experiencing, you would have peace through seeking God and acting in a way that glorifies Him.

Things happen in life, but remember there is no cloud that the sun cannot shine through…more importantly; there is no situation that God cannot fix. We just have to trust Him in it.

Be angry and do not sin; do not let the sun go down on your anger

Ephesians 4:26

Understanding the One Who Hurts

Last time that we discussed hurt, we took a look at the person who is hurt. We looked at what needs to be done in order to move forward from a place of being hurt. We discussed boundaries and the need for wise Counsel, as you are moving from the place of being hurt and offended to being free and forgiving.

Today, I want to take a look and the other side of that hurt coin. <u>The one who hurts.</u>

Now, if you have experienced being hurt and have not, whether you tried to or not, dealt with it in the proper manner, the pain of the hurt was able to seep into our heart. If this happened you allowed bitterness and anger to become wedged within the chambers of your heart. If this is true, you may have found that your actions, words, and even your thoughts have begun to change.

The truth is that we are all, in many ways, a product of our environment. The things, situations, and people that interact with us on a daily basis or even on an occurrence, have an opportunity to plant seed in to our hearts that can quickly take root. I believe that this is why God tells us in His word to guard our hearts with all diligence, (Proverbs 4:23) for out of it flows the issues of life. He didn't say that out of it will flow all of the great dreams of our lives. No, He said that our issues would come out of our hearts.

Not only will our issues come out of our hearts, but if there is goodness within us that will come out. Yet, if there is evil within us, that will come out too. When we are dealing with or have buried pain from hurtful situations, issues… they will also come out of our mouths.

For out of the abundance of the heart, the mouth speaks. (Luke 6:45)

If you take a moment to think about it, it is not only our actions that hurt people, but it is often our words, as well. We speak damaging words to other people, without even realizing that what we have said has the capacity to destroy them, in many ways. If we were to view things from God's eyes, we would see that our tongues are swords, cutting others on the way in and on the way out. Leave it to a heart that is hurting and the target will not only be broken, but demolished. If you can recognize yourself in these words, I want to tell you that you are not alone. It is just a sign that you are hurt.

Why?

Well, you've heard this before, but it's really true.

Hurt people, hurt people.

They do it unknowingly, most of the time. It starts with the pain that is within them and needs to be let go of, but because of unforgiveness, the hurt turns in to a weapon. In many ways, the hurt person is simply trying to protect herself from other forms of hurt, without realizing that the chosen weapon of protection is not a shield, but a sword. This is when problems arise.

If you have found yourself in this place, let me tell you that you don't have to stay here. Perhaps you have been hurting people, unawares. Maybe you aren't even to the place of hurting people yet. You are just thinking thoughts that if they came out of your mouth or would be acted upon, would hurt someone. If this is you, please, please keep reading.

The first thing to do is to declare that you will be honest with yourself and with God, no matter what you find out about yourself.

The second thing to do is to ask for forgiveness. You are asking forgiveness for hurting others. Next, forgive. Forgive yourself and the person/people that hurt you. You may have to go back to the situation and think about what happened. You may have to journal it and hash it out, but you need to get to the root of your problem, so that forgiveness can happen. Finally, you have to commit to renewing your mind and being a doer of the word.

God wants to bring about a change in your life, but He will not force His goodness upon your life, if you are not interested in having it. When you are a person that hurts others, you know that it comes from your past. It comes from your own brokenness. It comes from fear. It comes from desiring control. You have to be willing to let these things go in order to be set free.

If you are reading this, and don't quite understand this position, God bless you. However, I honestly believe that we have all been in a place like this, at one point in out lives or another. Maybe you could not recognize it, when in it. Maybe you did. We are all different, but I truly believe that we are all similar in this. None of us really want to remain in this place.

So, what's next?

Well, I suggest that you pray.

- <u>Pray</u> for the person that hurt you and pray for yourself.(Luke 6:28)
- <u>Trust God</u> to fight your battles. (Romans 12:19)
- <u>Renew</u> your mind daily. (Romans 12:2)
- <u>Practice</u> what you read and don't just read it.(James 1:22)

If you do these things, you will move from the place that you are in now, to the place where you desire to be, free from the pain and free to love.

*A man without self-control is like a city broken into and
left without walls.*
Proverbs 25:28

Your Emotions

Let's talk for a moment about the very busy and emotional ups and downs. The ups were about my day. The downs were about my past month. There were things that happened, conversations that I had, and questions that I asked, which are still on my mind.

Today, I realized, more than ever, that we may not get to choose the circumstances of our lives, but we do get to choose our reactions to them.

So this is what I want to share with you today.

Finally, brothers, whatever is true, whatever is honorable, whatever is just, whatever is pure, whatever is lovely, whatever is commendable, if there is any excellence, if there is anything worthy of praise, think about these things.
Philippians 4:8

The things that we think will help us act in a way that we can be proud of. The actions of others may cause us to consider doing things or saying things that are out of character, but prayer and proper thinking will help us to see life in a different light.

So try to make good decisions and have a good day.

*And which of you by being anxious can add single hour to
his span of life?*
Matthew 6:27

Stop Being Anxious and Fearful

What am I going to do?

I am not happy? I feel overwhelmed.

I have too much going on and I don't know how I am going to be able to do all of this.

What will tomorrow look like?

Will I be able to help my family?

Will they think I'm a failure?

What about me?

Where is my place in all of this?

These are questions that we all ask at some point in time in our lives. Sometimes we ask the questions and then continue to be productive in life. At other times, these questions cause us to begin to experience certain emotions within ourselves that are hard to get past. Whether we realize it or not, when we do not deal with these thoughts in the correct manner, they produce anxiety within us.

Anxiety in the heart of man causes depression, but a good word makes it glad. ~Proverbs 12:25

What is anxiety?

Anxiety is defined as...
a condition of mental uneasiness arising from fear or solicitude.

Very few of us can say that we have never experienced anxiety. From the moment that we begin to ask questions like, what am I going to do, and are not able to provide and answer, anxiety arises within us. We are uncertain about the future and become fearful because we have no confidence in the future of our lives or circumstances. As this happens, we become anxious.

anxious- deeply concerned, very solicitous; apprehensive.

That's right, we become deeply concerned. Our minds begin to wonder and we feel that we must do something to secure the future, so that we might feel more confident in what is to transpire in our lives.

apprehensive- fearful of evil; anxious for the future.

Not many of us do not want to admit that we are fearful. We don't want to say that we are fearful of evil. We don't want to admit that we are anxious about the future, but we might say that we are apprehensive at times. Yet, it is important that we truly understand what we are saying when we use words. When we say that we are apprehensive, we are admitting that we are fearful. We are admitting that we lack the confidence needed to walk courageously without anxiety.

solicitude- the state of being solicitous (eager, anxious, apprehensive, concerned); concerned; carefulness

These are the words that we can use to explain how we feel in an emotional state like this.

What does anxiety demonstrate?

More than we realize, our anxiety demonstrates that we are not trusting in God and more importantly, that we do not trust God.

Think about that for a moment.

Fear of the future is a direct indicator of our lack of trust in who God is and all that He has promised us.

Fear is apprehension of evil or danger; dread; anxiety; solicitude; to be in fear or feel anxiety.

God has said over and over again in the Bible that we should not fear. One example is in Joshua 1:9. Another is in Isaiah 41:10

Fear not, for I am with you;
Be not dismayed, for I am your God.
I will strengthen you,
Yes, I will help you,
I will uphold you with My righteous right hand

Did you get that? He said that He would take care of you. He told you that with His hand He would uphold you. Think about it. When we fear and are anxious, we lack trust in the words that God has said to us. We don't trust that He will keep His promises to us.

What has God said?

God has said over and over again that we should not fear. Yet we do. Even the Psalmists worried and were full of anxiety.

Psalm 94:16-18 *Who will rise up for me against the evildoers? Who will stand up for me against the workers of iniquity?*

Still, he had to bring himself back to a place of remembrance.

Unless the Lord had been my help,
My soul would soon have settled in silence.
If I say, "My foot slips,"
Your mercy, O Lord, will hold me up.

When we are going through struggles or feeling anxious, we find it hard to remember the things that God has done for us in the past. We forget words that God has said to us in that great love letter, the Bible. The awesome thing about God is that He never tires of giving us more direction.

And which of you by worrying can add one cubit to his stature? If you then are not able to do the least, why are you anxious for the rest? Consider the lilies, how they grow: they neither toil nor spin; and yet I say to you, even Solomon in all his glory was not arrayed like one of these. If then God so clothes the grass, which today is in the field and tomorrow is thrown into the oven, how much more will He clothe you, O you of little faith?
  "And do not seek what you should eat or what you should drink, nor have an anxious mind. For all these things the nations of the world seek after, and your Father knows that you need these things. But seek the kingdom of God, and all these things shall be added to you.
  "Do not fear, little flock, for it is your Father's good pleasure to give you the kingdom..." ~Luke 12:25-32

Man might not stand by His word. However, we are not talking about man. We are talking about the Almighty God.

By His word are the heavens upheld. (Hebrews 1:3: Genesis 1:3) By His word the sun shines and the moon gives us light at night. If He were to fail us, by not keeping His word…the whole world would fall apart…

This is why it is important for us to stop being anxious. We must trust in our God. We must have faith in who He is and what He has said He would do. (Hebrews 11:6) When we trust him, the health of our bodies will improve. Our bones will be stronger and we will not suffer depression. He has given us good words throughout the Bible, but we must have faith in Him in order for them to be of some help to us.

In short, I am say "Stop It!" You have the control and power to do it.

Therefore I tell you, do not be anxious about your life, what you will eat or what you will drink, nor about your body, what you will put on. Is not life more than food, and the body more than clothing?
Matthew 6:25

What do I need to know about anxiety?

I encouraged you to stop being anxious and fearful. I'm sure that I left you with a few questions, so now, I am going to tell you a few things you need to know about anxiety.

What is anxiety?

Anxiety is a state of mind where a person is concerned about something or someone. It has various ranges.

"It can go from genuine concern

For I have no man likeminded, who will naturally care for your state. ~Philippians 2:20

I sent him therefore the more carefully, that, when you see him again you may rejoice and that I may be less sorrowful ~Philippians 2:28

Beside those things that are without. That which cometh upon me daily. The care of all the churches ~2 Corinthians 11:28

to obsessions that originate from a distorted perspective of life."(source The Master Study Bible)

Matthew 6:25-34
Mark 4:19

Luke 12:22-31

How does anxiety sound, look, and feel?

The psalmists were great with expressing themselves. Through their thorough descriptions of life, we are able to look back the experiences that they had and become informed on various aspects of life. Anxiety is no different. They also felt anxiety and were very descriptive about how if affected them.

Psalm 94:16 Who will rise up for me against the evildoers? Or who will stand up for me against the workers of iniquity?

Psalm 38:6 I am troubled; I am bowed down greatly; I go mourning all day long.

Are you able to see what anxiety feels like? Is it similar to how you feel when you are anxious?

It is prohibited?

Did you know that God has told us not to be anxious?

Matthew 6:34 Take therefor no though for the morow for the morrow shall take thought for the things of itself. Sufficient unto the day is the evil thereof

Philippians 4:8 Be anxious for nothing, but in all things by prayer and supplication, with thanksgiving, let you requests be made known to God…

Luke 12:29 And do not seek what you should eat or drink, nor have an anxious mind.

Anxiety can be prevented.

Now we have already seen that God has told us not to be anxious, but it often doesn't feel that easy. In fact, it can feel down right impossible. Let's look at what the word of God says about preventing anxiety.

Seek first the kingdom of God and all of these things will be added to you ~Matthew 6:33

Everything that you are worried about will be taken care of if you seek first the kingdom of God.

Anxiety in the heart of man causes depression, but a good word makes it glad. Proverbs 12:25

Focusing on the wrong things will cause you to be anxious. Remember, anxiety is a state of mind. Therefore, you have to change your mind. Get a good word in you. Philipians 4:8

You can overcome anxiety
- 1 Peter 5:7
- Psalm 55:22
- Psalm 23:4
- Psalm 94: 19

I hope that you have found encouragement in this today. Trust God and walk in faith, free from anxiety.

Remember no one who puts their faith in God shall ever be put to shame Romans 10:11

Sleeplessness and the Struggle

"4:23 am. That's the time right now. I lie in bed, ready to go back to sleep after sitting here thinking and reading for 3 hours. I didn't wake up because I felt like it. I work up because my daughter wanted some water. After waking downstairs with her to get water, I found that I could not go back to sleep. I kept thinking of various topics. Books, stories, career paths, and my growling stomach echoed in my head, as I laid here as quiet and still as I could be. I don't want to wake anyone. I've been thinking about this whole career thing and it seems to me that the best thing for me to do right now is continue to work on my book and on being a writer. I have so many ideas and plans. I just need to make sure that I follow the Lord as I do all of these things."

We all have struggles. Some people struggle in their marriages. Some people struggle with their careers. Others struggle with parenting. I have met people that struggle with having too many friends and others that struggle with not having enough. Then, there are others, like me, who struggle with self.

Now this is a struggle that digs very deep because, if I am to be very honest with you, which it is my aim to be, struggling with the person that is with you all of the time is not an easy thing. Ha!

That's right! I am with me all of the time and whatever it is that I struggle with do not just go away. It cannot be ignored and I definitely cannot just sweep it under the rug. Instead, my issues with myself nag at me night and day.

Now, you might understand my struggle, as most people do. When it balls down to it, all of our relational issues start somewhere. They start within us and in our relationship to God.

When we have marital issues, there are certain things that we have allowed to take place in our relationships that required is to set boundaries that were not set; and while this is sometimes the case, I have to truthful about the fact that this is not always the case. Perhaps, like many people a person that struggles with their marriage, finds herself unhappily married to her husband. She searches herself and wonders, "How did we get here? How did I get here?" She takes all of the problems of the marriage, and not matter how much she says that he is the problem, she internalize the issues. She tried to change something about herself, thinking that she is the problem. Deep down, her struggle becomes apparent. He is struggling with herself. She longs for a satisfaction that she is not receiving from her marriage, but should she be receiving it from that source or from another Source...God?

The struggle with receiving satisfaction from the Source continues to ooze into every area of life as it can be found in the career, mothering, building relationships with other women, and even more so, but dealing with self.

My struggle is all too common and as I live with the stifle, I find that it seems to appear in everything that I do. They all become infected with problem-with-self-a-tosis. I expect too much from myself. I set really high standards and then freak myself out to the point where I am stuck trying to meet my own standard. I push myself too hard and convince myself that everything I do should be, well...perfect. This issue that I face within myself is not one that stops with myself. It leaks into all of my relationships and activities.

There is a constant pressure that is felt to do it all the right way all of the time. This is one of my biggest struggles. It's because I don't want to miss the mark...you know...**sin**.

I guess that's my real struggle. Remember that I told you earlier that the struggle with self intimately turns into a struggle with God. Now can you see it? Do you see how this all filters into everything that we do and every relationship that we have?

Some people hold a very low standard for themselves, while others, like me, hold a very high standard. While the standard is not the issue, the level of realistic-ness, is an issue

Side note: yes, I have created a few words in this chapter in order to accurately communicate what I am trying to say to you.

How do we get a realistic idea of the standard? That answer comes through our relationship with God and His Word.

While I do read the Bible and pray, there are times in life, where the cares of this life try to crowd out all of the details that the Holy Spirit has given me through the Word. There are times when my time with God should be better spent listening instead of petitioning Him for my requests.

There are moments when my time in life should be spent more on being instead of doing. When I do these things, I receive a clear standard. I am able to see what I can realistically do. I am able to have a realistic standard for my relationships and affairs in life.

Why? The reason for this is that my vision becomes God-led instead of self-led.

This process is something that we must go through daily in order to be at a place where we are satisfied with life. Not only should, being God-led is a daily thing, but it should also be a moment by moment thing...

His Presence and Guidance should be the air that we breathe. In this our issues with self will become a bit different because God will help us to deal with us. The word will help to put it under subjection and thus, our relationships and endeavors will benefit from our relationship with God.

I know that I am not perfect, but because I want to be pleasing to God, I aim very high. I realize that my standard and His are very different thus my issue with myself, more than anything else that I have mentioned is submission to His will. Not only in word, but in deed and expectation. Will I allow my standard to supersede His? Will I measure my relationships according to my standard or His? Will my career meet my expectation or His? Will my desire for order reach my expectation or His?

...Because truth be told, my standard could never meet His standard. His ways are higher than mine and no matter how much I attempt to elevate my standard; this level of perfection cannot meet His level of expectation.

When I submit my way to His, His purpose is fulfilled, relationships are blessed, people are changed, hopes and dreams are satisfied, and I sleep well...and this, my friend is why I believe that our struggle is constant. The more we live and breathe; we will struggle with ourselves in order to convince ourselves that it is ultimately God's way and not ours.

Can you relate to the struggles that I have presented here? Do you find that all of your struggles ball down to your struggle with yourself and God? Take a moment to be honest with yourself about your struggle with yourself and how it affects your life?

I pray that, like me, you would find that God is always there to help and to love on you. Remember, He knows you better than anyone and He is patiently working in you to see His will accomplished in your life.

"Let us go to the Jordan and each of us get there a log and let us make a place for us to dwell there." And he answered, "Go."
2 Kings 1:7

Where do I Fit In?

There are times where you know where you fit it. Then there are times when you don't. This weekend I spent some time looking at the world, my life, and ministry.

As I looked and thought, I wondered where I fit in. I started thinking about the big picture and how God wants to use me.

God has placed, in each one of us, gifts and talents. He has given us to our families, friends, ministries, and the world. Yet, we cannot do it all, all of the time.

I say this because there are times, when I want to do it all and be all to all people, but truth be told, that is now wise nor possible.

I have to look at the things that are going on in my life and be prayerful about how God desires for me to be productive in a situation.

All of this thinking, for a short time, caused me to feel like I had no place. I saw myself as a speck of sand on a beach full of sand…where did I fit in and what was the point…

I saw all of the problems of the world and wanted to be a part of the solutions. I saw all of the pain and wanted to be a part of the healing. I wanted to be a help…

Here's what I mean…

I don't just want to be a replica of some other mother, wife, woman…I want to be who God created me to be. In all of my uniqueness…and I am very unique and still I am commonly, uncommon…I stand out in various ways that are not always comfortable. This caused me to ask…should I be? Should I stand out because I am just like the others or should I be comfortable being uncomfortable because I stand out as me…just the way God created me to be?

I hope this makes sense because I am not trying to confuse you.

I want you to know, as I am realizing, that God has called each one of us to be very different in this world. We may have certain qualities or circumstances that are similar to our sisters in Christ, or even have some stories that the other women in the world may relate to, but we are not supposed to look like, sound like, and dress like them.

Our identity must rest in Christ. This must be our resting place…a place of comfort.

As I thought of these things, I felt inadequate…as if I could not handle those things that God has brought me to handle. I had, for a brief moment lost my sight. I could not see where I fit in…

But God…

As I thought...I contemplated...I read my Bible...I prayed...I waited...and I prayed some more...

He reminded me that I fit in Him. He is my source and my purpose. He is the reason why I am alive and my reason for being. I had to stop thinking on how big the world was and all that was going on in it and focus on how great my God is. Realizing His awesomeness, allowed me to grasp hold of his purpose for me...

In this I rested...

As I rested, it was revealed.

Perfectionism is not the way to go.

Being like everyone else is not the way to go.

Being recommended or recognized...even honored, are not the ways to go.

The way to go is by His grace, as I trust His leading...

In that moment, as I dwelled on Him...I was at peace. I could see that none of my own expectations or the expectations of the world may add up, but His will...would.

In this...I found peace.

I realized, through His revelation that all of the things that He reveals to me through various avenues, He will put to use, in time…

What He gives me to use, when He gives me to use it…can be utilized, as long as I trust in Him…

In this, I heard His voice…

Calling me to listen harder and pay attention amongst all of the noise…

In Him…I found my place in all of this

So she called the name of the Lord who spoke to her, "You are a God of seeing" for she said, "Truly here I have seen Him who looks after me."
Genesis 16:13

Just Be You

Being original isn't hard, but for some reason, we all struggle at it a little bit. We look around and see certain things working for some people and other things working for others. We wonder, "could any of this work for me."

Without saying no, I am saying that it is extremely critical that we realize the importance in being unique.

Out of all the people in the world, there are no two that share the same fingerprint. That says a lot. Although we all have eyes and they range from green, to blue, to brown...no two people have the same iris or retinal pattern.

I would bet that if we were to count the number of hairs on our heads, we would find that we differ there as well. What does this say about our Maker? What does this say about us?

Well, from where I'm sitting, it says that He likes variety and uniqueness. It says that being special is not found in our commonality, but in our uniqueness.

This makes sense because some people wonder how God could find you, me, and 50,000 others special. The truth is we are all special in different ways. He looks at us and sees who we are and that is what makes us special.

We each make Him laugh a certain way. We get His attention and touch His heart in a certain way…
Do you see where I am going with this?

Our family and friends feel the same way, even if they never say it. They see how unique and special we are and their hearts smile…

I am saying all of this to help you, and me, walk upright with our heads held high because we are, in our uniqueness, great.

So stop trying to be like the other gal and just be you…

Draw near to God, and He will draw near to you. Cleanse your hands, you sinners, and purify your hearts, you double minded
James 4:8

Feeling Overwhelmed

We all have these days…

You know them…

Days where it's hard to move forward…

Hard to smile…

Hard to function…

Not because of the weather, or something that just happened, but because something is bothering you…

Something is causing you to be emotional…

Something that makes you want to quit…

To say, "I'm done."

It makes you vulnerable and turns everything else into a big deal too…

Capable of snapping on someone…

You hold back…

Shut down…

Pull back the tears…

And run inside where no one but God can see you…

And while there…you say…

"God why?!"

Everyone around you thinks they know, but they have no clue…

If you are like me, you realize…

THIS IS OVERWHELMING!!!

STOP!!! STOP RIGHT THERE!!!

What is the problem? Who is the problem? Why is there a problem? Why such great turmoil, pain, agony…Why?

We don't wrestle against flesh and blood…No

We wrestle against the principalities in this life, against rulers, against the powers, against the world forces in this darkness, against the spiritual forces of wickedness in the heavenly places…

That's what Ephesians 6:12, 13 says.

They make themselves known and affect us by whispering things in our ears, throwing destructive darts at our minds, and aiming their blows at our hearts...

But we have a choice...

Say this with me...

OVERWHELMED!!! YES, I AM OVERWHELMED!!!!

I am overwhelmed with emotions, but I will decide why I am overwhelmed... and it is not because of what these forces have to dish out against me...

NO!!!

I am overwhelmed because I serve a great God that is more than able to take care of me and everything that attempts to overwhelm me.

I am overwhelmed because of His great salvation. I am overwhelmed because of His love. I am overwhelmed because of His heart for me.

I am overwhelmed because of His power and His might...

I am overwhelmed because in the midst of my emotions, He makes Himself known...through the trees, the wind...

Through the birds...

Through the color of everything around me...

He whispers in my heart...

FEAR NOT!!! I AM HERE AND I HAVE ALREADY OVERCOME THEM!!! HAVE COURAGE AND HOLD ON TO ME...I AM HERE AND I'VE GOT THIS...

You just don't know how completely overwhelmed I am right now...

I can feel His love...can you?

In the mist of my brokenness...in the midst of my ache...I know He is all-powerful.

My husband said "Don't let anyone mess up your day! Have a good one..."

That was God, speaking through Him...

The "let" in his statement said "take authority...don't let it have power over you...put on the armor of God and stand"

Today, I stand on my knees...worshiping HIM.

I will choose what overwhelms me. It will not be the cares of this life, or the problems...or the people...It will be God! He will overwhelm me...

Have you ever felt overwhelmed?

How do you handle it?

Are you able to take control of your emotions and focus on Him?

Try it! Next time let Him overwhelm you…it may take a minute, but whisper "God help me to be overwhelmed by you." and I promise you will experience a great and powerful overwhelming that you will yearn for again…

Casting all your anxieties on him, because h cares for you
1 Peter 5:7

Don't Forget to Breathe

Have you ever had a moment when you found yourself gasping for air? No, I don't mean literally, but you can feel it. It seems like everything around you is going so fast that you just can't seem to catch your breath.

I know that you know what I'm talking about. It's that time in your life when you feel like you are spinning around in circles, getting dizzy, and are about to pass out because you aren't getting enough oxygen to your brain.

Those are the times when it is imperative for us to take time away. It might be a vacation. It could be a day. It could be as simple as a few minutes out of the time that you spend being super busy. Where ever you make the time to do it, that time becomes your point of rejuvenation.

How do I know? Well, it's simple. I've been there. I've been at a point before where I was trying to be everything to everybody. I thought that being a good woman, friend, and Christian meant that I had to say "yes!" and do it all…all the time.

That's when, thankfully, God's Holy Spirit stepped in and began to tell me something that I will never forget.

BREATHE...Don't forget to breath

Hearing those words caused me to feel like someone cared about all that I had been experiencing and that I was important too. I began to realize that I didn't have to pour out everything in order to be the woman that I believed that God had created me to be. It was OK to slow down or stop at a point when I knew that it was too much. I became more encouraged as I felt the Holy Spirit unction me to say "No, I'm sorry. I understand, but the answer is no."

Today my life is a bit more balanced. I am no longer the same woman that I once was. I know, now, how to say no.

So, why am I writing this?

I'm writing this because I believe that it is important to share my story so that I can help someone else. If you are reading this and life seems to be moving at the speed of lighting, take a moment and breathe.

Find time throughout your day, week, month, and year to simply look up at the clouds or the sky...the trees, the stars...watch the kids play and as you do, remember to breathe.
Thank God for all you have and all He is in your life. Put one foot in front of the other and continue to move forward. I hope you found comfort and encouragement in this.

The God who equipped me with strength and made my way blameless
Psalm 18:32

5 Reasons Why You Don't Always Have to Be Strong

My entire adult life, I have been married and a mother. I had to mature very quickly in order to fulfill my role as mother and wife. I remember when I was a child, I wanted to hurry up and become a grown woman. I didn't know that it would come so soon.

However, when the time came, I stepped into my shoes as mother and wife. I did my best in everything and I learned how to be strong. Over time, being strong began to take a toll on me.

My friends seemed to think that I didn't need encouragement or a helping hand because; I was always doing those things for them.

It wasn't that I didn't need it. It was something completely different.

When I was in the first year of my marriage and had just had my son, I had an encounter. This encounter would begin to shape my life for years and I didn't understand why until recently.

At this vulnerable and very impressionable stage in my life, I turned to a minister that I thought could help me. I thought he would lead my husband and I, as we traveled the road of learning to be great parents and spouses. In my heart, I longed for a word that would show us how to walk with God and with one another.

This leader would speak into my life at various points. I remember going to him because I had found that I was different from my peers at the time. They were all single and doing things that 20 year olds do. However, I was a mother and a wife. I was in the military and I owned my own home. I had more in common with the 30 and 40-year-old women, than I did with the women that were my age. His advice to me was simple. *He said show yourself friendly. If you want a friend be a friend.*

That is exactly what I did. I was there for people as I had wanted them to be there for me, but when I needed them, they were not there.

I have to admit that their unavailability, allow God to be there for me more and more. However, I began to build up this aspect of myself that had to be strong because if I became weak, no one would be able to help my friends and my friends wouldn't be able to help me.

I couldn't understand why thing were this way, but I never gave it any thought until one day. My family and I were over 2,500 miles away in a new state. I didn't know anyone and no one knew me. I started thinking about all of my relationships and my desire to have people in my life that genuinely cared for me as much as I did for them. I saw that when I was strong and helpful, people clung to me. However, I also began to realize that those types of relationships were not healthy for myself of my friends, so I began to make some changes.

When my friends would call, I would listen more. When they awaited my answer to their problem, I asked them questions about what they were going to do.

At the time I was also going through some training as a Rehabilitation Counselor and I was learning that there is power is asking questions that are not leading. I started telling myself that in order to truly build up my friends, I had to back off and allow God to do His work through the Holy Spirit in their lives. I could not solve everything for them.

Setting Boundaries
I stopped answering the phone at 2 o'clock in the morning and worrying about how they were going to fix their lives. Instead, I fell on my knees and I prayed for them.

When I wasn't able to handle their lack of desire to do and be better, I said so and then asked them what they wanted me to do to help them. If their expectations where what I could handle, I did it. If they weren't, I simply stated this. I had to make sure that my friends understood that I was being strong for them, but in another way. I was setting some healthy boundaries.

Do you know what happened?

My friends started to grow up. They no longer expected me to be strong and they began to make better choices in their own lives.

Thinking on this helped me to realize that so many women are always trying to be strong. We are strong because it is always projected that in order to be great you have to be the stronger one.

Why do we fight it?
In our society, it is never encouraged to be the weaker vessel. Why?

They say that only the strong survive. They also tell us that what we want is to survive. Well, I want to challenge that thought. I want to thrive. Not only do I want to thrive, but I want to live because I am alive. I am not dead and avoiding death is not the sole purpose of my life. This is why so many women have trouble submitting to their husbands. They feel that if they submit, it means that they are weak.

YES!!! It does. It means that you and I are the weaker vessel in our marriages. We should be proud of that fact. What woman, honestly, wants to be married to a man that is weaker than she is? He could not protect her or their family. She would have to do it all.

If we are to be honest, in order to thrive as a married couple…be prosperous and develop well, as a married couple, we all have to love each other well.

Do you know that it wasn't until I took this stand in ALL of my relationships that my quality of life began to improve?

Here are the 5 things that I learned.

1. Always being strong drains you

I found that being strong left me with little energy. I had to be strong enough to listen to people's problems and to solve them. I had to be strong enough to take what they threw my way and not flinch. I had to always be ready. This was tiring.

2. If you are always strong, you leave no power for God's strength

You have probably heard this before, but I am going to tell you again. God has given us strength for this life, but He also knows that there will be specific points, where He will need to be strong for us. These times allow Him to show us how much He cares for us.

"For the sake of Christ, then, I am content with weaknesses, insults, hardships, persecutions, and calamities. For when I am weak, then I am strong." 2 Corinthians 2:10

Yet when we cover up our weakness and pretend to be strong through it all, we leave no room for Him to be God in our lives. In our strength, we tell Him, "I don't need You to be strong for me."

3. Being strong all of the time tells everyone else in your world that you don't need them

Just like our strength communicates to God that we don't need Him, other people in our lives begin to receive the same message. They feel that they are not strong enough to help us because we have it all taken care of. We make them think that we are super human, when in reality; we struggle just like they do.

4. Always being strong can lead to pride and pride leads to a fall

When we are always strong, we can begin to fool ourselves in to thinking that we don't need anyone. We feel that no one is capable of helping us and with this, pride begins to move into our lives. Pride can be very dangerous because it takes away our ability to see all of the needs that we have. The only way for us to recognize those needs is for something to happen, the fall…

5. It might be someone else's turn

Have you ever thought that perhaps your strength was standing in the way of someone else being strong? I didn't until it happened to me. I had a friend that was really strong. She was so strong that she would not let me help her. I had never been that way, but her actions caused me to wonder if my other friends had perceived me as such. I waited a while for an opportunity to show her how much I cherished our friendship, but that opportunity never arrived. I had asked to help and volunteered, but she never would take any type of help, encouragement, or friendly gesture of caring through gifts.

This relationship showed me that sometimes it's just not our turn to be strong. It might be someone else's turn to be strong and we need to back off. From then on, I wanted to do my best to allow my friends to be strong for me and I would continue to do the same thing, when needed.

If you don't get anything else out of this, I want you to know that you don't have to do it all or be it all to everyone. All you have to do is be you and give this life all that you've got. Your strength is not who you are. It is a quality that you possess. It also does not define you. You are so much more than one word, strong. There is great value in you, but in order for you to see it; you're going to have to step out of your own strength and into God's strength. There is a time and place for everything. Just know that when you decide you don't want to be strong, there is still greatness in you.

Scriptures to Read & Prayers to Pray for Yourself as a Woman

Anyone that's been reading this blog for a while or knows me knows that I enjoy encouraging people. Many times in my life when I needed some encouragement, there was no one to be found, besides family, of course.

Yet, I longed for more.

I wanted to be able to sit down with a girlfriend and discuss the troubles that I was facing. I wanted someone that could encourage me and not just let me wallow in the mud. Instead what I found was a great friend in God. He showed me how much He cared for me and how much He thought of me.

Why do I say that? Well, if we look at the Scriptures, it becomes evident that God had us on His mind as the Bible was being written. For a long time, it was a part of my Christian emergency on the go kit. (before the Bible app) I quickly learned that if I needed encouragement, I had to encourage myself through the Holy Spirit and the Word of God.

So today, I want to share a few of my favorite scriptures to read and pray with you. By no means are these all of them, just a few that I want to share for today.

Romans 10:11 For the scripture says, Whosoever believes on him shall not be ashamed. (When I needed boldness to stand on God's word)

Hebrews 11:6 But without faith it is impossible to please him: for he that comes to God must believe that he is, and that he is a rewarder of them that diligently seek him. (When I needed to understand how to go to God and what He expected of me)

Matthew 19:26 But Jesus beheld them, and said to them, With men this is impossible; but with God all things are possible (When I needed to know that God could do the impossible and that I could trust Him to do just that)

Matthew 6:33 But seek you first the kingdom of God, and his righteousness; and all these things shall be added unto you. (When I needed to know that God would take care of me, so I could seek His face and work in His kingdom without worrying about my needs and wants)

Isaiah 54: 4 Fear not; for you shall not be ashamed: neither be you confounded; for you shall not be put to shame: for you shall forget the shame of your youth, and shall not remember the reproach of your widowhood any more. (When I was afraid of what was to come and of what would be said about what happened)

Isaiah 54:5 For your Maker is your husband; the LORD of hosts is his name; and your Redeemer the Holy One of Israel; The God of the whole earth shall he be called. (When my heart was broken)

Isaiah 54: 13 And all your children shall be taught of the LORD; and great shall be the peace of your children. (Whenever I was concerned for my children)

Isaiah 54:17 No weapon that is formed against you shall prosper; and every tongue that shall rise against you in judgment you shall condemn. This is the heritage of the servants of the LORD, and their righteousness is of me, says the LORD. (When I am concerned about what others will say)

I really love all of Isaiah 54…it really speaks to me

Psalm 91:5-12 (for overall protection) *You shall not be afraid for the terror by night; nor for the arrow that flies by day; Nor for the pestilence that walks in darkness; nor for the destruction that wastes at noonday. A thousand shall fall at your side, and ten thousand at your right hand; but it shall not come near you. Only with your eyes shall you behold and see the reward of the wicked. Because you have made the LORD, who is my refuge, even the most High, your habitation; There shall no evil befall you, neither shall any plague come near your dwelling. For he shall give his angels charge over you, to keep you in all your ways. They shall bear you up in their hands, lest you dash your foot against a stone.*

Psalm 34 (The entire chapter) *verse 4: I sought the LORD, and he heard me, and delivered me from all my fears.* (I needed to be reminded that the Lord hears me); *verses 8-10* (the promise of God for my personal needs and wants); *O taste and see that the LORD is good: blessed is the man that trusts in him.; O fear the LORD, you his saints: for there is no lack to them that fear him. The young lions do lack, and suffer hunger: but they that seek the LORD shall not lack any good thing.*

Psalm 2:8 Ask of me, and I shall give thee the heathen for thine inheritance, and the uttermost parts of the earth for thy possession. (When I would pray for people to get saved. A reminder that God would hear me and His promise to act)

1 Peter 5:7 Casting all your care upon him; for he cares for you. (A constant reminder that God cares about everything the I care about…all of it)

James 5:14-16 (A reminder of the power of prayer) *Is any sick among you? let him call for the elders of the church; and let them pray over him, anointing him with oil in the name of the Lord: And the prayer of faith shall deliver the sick, and the Lord shall raise him up; and if he has committed sins, they shall be forgiven him. Confess your faults one to another, and pray one for another, that you may be healed. The effectual fervent prayer of a righteous man avails much.*

James 4:8 Draw near to God, and he will draw near to you. Cleanse your hands, you sinners; and purify your hearts, you double-minded. (When I want to draw near to God, He wants to draw near to me too)

2 Timothy 2:15 Study to shew thyself approved unto God, a workman that needeth not to be ashamed, rightly dividing the word of truth. (Encouragement and reason to study…this scripture was the foundation for my Bible study life)

As I said before, these are not all of my favorites, but the ones that came to my heart to share right now. Say these scriptures and pray them frequently. I know that they will help and encourage you.

Pray without ceasing…

Being a Wife

Who can find a virtuous wife?
For her worth is far above rubies.
Proverbs 31:10

Marriage...

The sacred bond between a man and a woman ordained by God and recognized by the law & the church.

Marriage is another one of God's institutions that is under siege by its unseen enemy.

If you are a married woman, then you are a wife. You are the female half of this whole. You are the part of this union that bears children with the pain of child-birth. You are the part of this union that submits to the head of the household because you believe that he is led by God. You are the part of the household that supports the heart of her husband and prays for the weaknesses that he has, which no one else, besides the Lord, can see. You are his help-meet.

If you are a wife, you must realize that there is a very real, unseen enemy out there. He goes by the name of divorce, adultery, confusion, and destruction of marriage. The Bible calls him our adversary and enemy of our souls.

If you are reading this, you are probable wondering where I am going with this, because you are aware of what I am saying already. I just want to take a moment to remind you that you have the power, within your marriage to uphold your marriage vows. You have the power to strengthen your husband through prayer. You have the ability to stand strong on behalf of a people that are breaking apart at the seams because of an unseen enemy that has come up against marriage; Not only yours, but mine.

I want to remind you that when you stand in pray for marriage, you do not stand alone. God is there with you and so am I. I want to remind you that fear is your enemy. Do not be afraid of tactics that our adversary, the devil, brings your way.

Recognize that God is more powerful; He is stronger; He is greater than anyone or anything that could ever come up against your marriage. You just have to trust Him. He has a plan for your marriage. He has a purpose for your marriage. Your marriage has a hope and a future, so don't give up. And if you are already standing strong, grab ahold of another wife and help her to be strong, right along with you.

This is just a little reminder from one wife to another.

> *Wives, likewise, be submissive to your own husbands, that even if some do not obey the word, they, without a word, may be won by the conduct of their wives,*
>
> ~1 Peter 3:1

Being a Wise Married Woman

What type of wife are you?

When you sit down and evaluate the place that your marriage is in relative to where it was 6 months ago or even a year ago, what would you say about its progress? Would you say that there has been any progress? Would you say that there has been regression or that it has been stagnant? What would your husband say about your relationship? What would he say about you as a wife?

Now, up until this point we have discussed being a woman and the importance of not allowing the opinions of men to be the overwhelming factor of your decisions. While this is still true, this is one area that you have to consider the opinion of a man. That man is your husband.

My husband and I have been married for 15 years and we have really grown. In the first few years of our marriage, I was plagued by worry and fear of all the wicked and evil things that had happened in my family's past. I hoped for the good, but wondered if God was really going to keep us from the big "D" word…DIVORCE.

If my husband and I were to sit down with you and your husband to be honest about where we were 13 years ago, we would say that we were in a rough spot. We were deeply in love, but marriage was hard.

We had both been raised by single parents and had no idea of how a married couple should communicate, work together, and support one another. You add in being fresh out of high school, parents, in the military, and new homeowners, life was very stressful.

I was afraid that he was going to cheat on me, abuse me, and leave me high & dry without out a pot to potty in. (You know that's not really what they say, but you get the picture.) I had said that I had given him my heart, but the truth was that I was anxiously afraid that giving him all of me would leave none of me.

When I say all of me, I do not mean making him my god. I just mean loving him whole heartedly and trusting that he would always be there for me.
I struggled with my own insecurities and wondered if he despised me. I was always concerned if he was looking to another woman to fulfill his needs and my actions showed it.

This lack of trust and faith in him, our love, our relationship, and God, filtered through our entire household. We argued a lot and I was afraid to submit. Truth be told, I didn't know how. I had never seen a woman married to a man, happily married. I didn't know what it meant for a man to love his wife and not desire another woman.

Everything I had seen, to include in the media taught me that marriage was a toss-up. You could win or lose and you should know that the odds were that you would lose. However, that treasure that God had given me began to talk to me. I prayed and asked God for direction. I wasn't happy and my husband wasn't happy. How were we going to make it? He was my high school sweetheart and I desperately wanted us to make it.

Nana said that I had to pray. See one of my concerns was that I had grown up in the church and my husband hadn't. I felt alone spiritually and wasn't sure how to get him on board. Instead of praying, like Nana said, I nagged my husband.

I wanted him to be at church, so I nagged him about that. I wanted him to read the Bible, so I nagged him about that too. I didn't want to feel alone anymore, but looking back on it, I didn't trust God to fix it, so I nagged.

I was serving in church and very busy. I was there every time that the doors were open. I was doing what the bible said about praying for my spouse and I was trying to be humble, but if I am to be honest with you, I was indignant and showed no respect for my husband. He could see it and feel it. This is not an excuse, but I didn't know what respect meant as a newly married woman.

One Saturday evening after prayer, a woman that I highly respect came to me and said something that really got under my skin. She said, "You know, you are at church too much. Why don't you consider staying home with your husband sometime?" This upset me to my core. This woman had no understanding of how badly I needed God, but at that time, I was confused too. I thought that God was in the church and that as long as I served the church, he would fix my marriage.

Sadly, to say, for years after that I continued to work hard in the church, while failing my husband. Then Nana said something to me in one of our conversations. "Keda, a sanctified wife MAKES a sanctified husband." She emphasized this as she said it over and over again. Desperate for answers, I looked up this scripture. I needed the answer, so I studied it. I begin to learn that two people, when married become one. That meant that if one person was so saturated with the love of God, the other would be too. I wanted my husband with me in this, so I began to ask God to sanctify my husband.

Do you know what the Lord said to me?

I first had to sanctify myself.

What? I thought I was sanctified. I thought I was righteous. I could not see my faults and failures as a wife and help-meet. I was so indoctrinated by the world that marriage wasn't working for me because…I was prideful. I thought that I could rule my husband with an iron fist and the truth is that my husband was stronger that I could ever be. The more I pushed him, the harder he pushed back, so I decided to try it God's way.

I began to submit myself to God and to allow Him to change me. I kept my Bible with me, like we carry around our phones. I read it day and night. I prayed all of the time. I got up early in the morning, prayed, and read my Bible. I wanted this change so bad that I began to get lost in God.

That's when he began to change me. I was turning from all of the evil things and thoughts that I had grown up with and as I changed, so did my husband. As we changed, so did our relationship.

I had to learn that I could not be the head of the house because a body with two heads is deformed. I not only had to humbly myself before my husband, but I had to be willing to trust God. I had to know that He was not going to fail me.

So, I made a decision. After 5 years of being with my husband, arguing and fighting for years, ready to give up and be divorced, I cried out to God. Do you know what He said?

"You have to make a choice."

What did he mean?

Let me tell you.

I wanted my husband to be 100% committed, but I had one foot in the door and the other one outside of it. I was ready to leave at the drop of a dime, but I expected my husband to stick around no matter what. So, God was telling me that I had straddled the fence enough in my marriage and needed to get settled in.

That's when I made the decision. I had already said that I only wanted to be married one time, but I had not told myself that divorce was not an option. I had said the normal things that 21st century women say. "If he cheats on me, I'm gone." Then I searched for evidence of it, hoping never to find it and praying that God would fix us.

What a mess I was…double minded in my ways. That's why my prayers weren't getting answered. The bible says that I should have even expected anything from God because I was so confused myself.

I thought of what Nana had said and I considered what the Lord had placed in my heart and I and I made a decision. I decided that I was going to trust the Lord 100% with my marriage and with my heart. I told my husband that I wasn't going anywhere and was in the marriage for life. I explained that from that moment forward, divorce wasn't an option, unless the Lord showed me otherwise. Honestly, I couldn't think of any situations where the Lord would tell me to leave my husband, but I'm sure that there are marriages that have endured situations that deem separation at some point. If not, the Lord would not have allowed it in the New Testament.

From the moment that I made that decision, being a wife became easier for me. I looked to God as to how I was supposed to fulfill my husband in various areas of our relationship. I prayed diligently for God to fix things and for Him to change me because I knew that my change would bring about an eventual change in my husband.

I began to see service to my husband as service to God. I recognized the value that God had placed on my vow to say. He saw that I was standing on the word of God and He blessed me.

Our relationship hasn't been all hunky dory, but it has gotten a lot better. I used to say that I wanted my husband to be my best friend and today, outside of the Lord and my oldest two friends that I've had, He is. I tell more than I tell anyone else. He listens to me and when prays for me.

I am ever thankful for the wise words of my grandmother and for the patience of God. He gave us a chance. I know that we had other issues, but I want you to understand that I only had the power to change myself. I had to give myself over to God in submission and complete trust. I had to know that He would hear my prayers and work things out for my marriage.

In the beginning, I wasn't a good wife or a wise woman married woman, but today I believe that by the grace of God that I am.

The wise woman builds her house,

But the foolish pulls it down with her hands.

Proverbs 14:1

A Foolish Woman

Have you ever read a portion of scripture that showed you yourself?

One day, while reading the Bible I came across a scripture. Proverbs 9:13

"A foolish woman is clamorous; She is simple, and knows nothing."

When I read this I wondered what clamorous meant. After looking it up, I found the word boisterous. The definition of boisterous is a person, event, or behavior that is noisy, energetic, and rowdy. I was a cheerleader in high school so reading this word caused me to do the cheer in my head. R-O-double-U-D-Y. Then there was a word that I did not like, unrestrained.

When I meditated on this scripture and though on what these words meant, I thought of the type of woman that I used to be. As a wife I was loud, never toning it down to be humble or to listen to my husband. Whenever, I had a problem, I didn't know how to address him in love with respect.

For this very reason, we argued…a lot. When we did he would tell me that I was a disrespectful woman. I couldn't see it through.

What I could see was the error of his ways. I could see his lack of desire to communicate and listen to me. What I failed to see what that my lack of respect translated and communicated through everything that I said and did.

So honestly, how could I respect any respectful communication between the two of us?

I was a foolish woman and I'm thankful that God place it in my heart to seek wisdom. As I did, I began to see and understand the issues at hand…my issues.

Proverbs 7:11

"She was loud and rebellious, her foot would not stay at home."

This scripture brought to mind the things that I would do. I would yell, scream, holler, and fuss. I wanted to burn up the road all of the time. I was at my college, out selling Mary kay, at the church, visiting friends…I wasn't happy at home and was trying to stay preoccupied, but if I had sought wisdom I would have seen and understood that happiness at home first starts by being there.

The woman at the church told me that I should stay home with him sometimes. Like a scoffer, I laughed within and rejected her wisdom, the wisdom of God. I thought my healing would come from church. I didn't realize that God could heal my broken heart through fellowship with Him and my husband. Together, they had the capacity to heal me.

Now here I am 15 years after saying "I do" and I understand. When we discern wisdom, we become wise. When we hear from the Lord and are willing to consider what He says, we can begin to walk in wisdom. When we are wise, we don't do what I did in the past, shun wisdom immediately.

My prayer has continually been that God would help me to be a wise woman and not a scoffer. I desire to hear wisdom, when He speaks and understand knowledge when I receive it.

Let all bitterness and wrath and anger and clamor and slander be put away from you, along with all malice. Be kind to one another, tenderhearted, forgiving one another, as God in Christ forgave you.

~Ephesians 4:31,32

Marriage and Issues

Sometimes married people get into arguments over the dumbest things. As they argue, they find that the smallest issues are brought up and turned into mountains in their relationship; mountains that seemingly can't be moved.

It's so sad because it's not worth all the trouble over something so small and petty. They call each other names, curse, scream, and holler...and for what?! No one has the answer.

They are really trying to address another issue that has absolutely nothing to do with the topic at hand. It they would just discuss that particular issue; things would be fine. Both parties would be able to see the others perspective and perhaps do something to fix the issue.

This knowledge that I have did not come from reading a book, nor is it a theory. I know this from my first-hand experience with my husband. We have come to a place where we are able to address complex issues without talking about the mundane issues that occurred. There is no need to cover up feelings. The best thing to do is, simply, be honest with one another. This fixes a lot.

I wish a newly married couple all the best and recommend that they remain open, honest, and loving towards one another.

Learning to have open, honest, and loving communication is not easy. You look at your husband and see his flaws, errors, and mistakes. You look in the mirror at that same moment and find yourself flawless. I know that I've done this before.

He pinpoints something that I don't want to look at and deal with and I'm frustrated. He makes a comment about something and I'm wondering why he had to say something in the first place.

I talk and he seems not to be listening, yet later on he can quote me verbatim. I what change that he's not willing to make, conversations that he doesn't want to have and now, we are both frustrated. Frustration about the kids, the finances, the house, the housework, the movie, the car…you name it, we could get frustrated about it.

The truth is that this is what real relationships are like. Two people growing together in a marriage experience scuffs, bumps, and hiccups as they become one. We each have to rid ourselves of habits that are unhealthy. Sometimes as an individual, we don't see them and neither does he. Yet, bringing them up puts them on the radar.

No one really wants to hear what's wrong with them, especially from a spouse, but this is how progress and change happen. My husband says that we are not the people that we were when we first got married and that's a good thing. I agree with him. I am better and so is he. Those changes didn't happen overnight.

They happened with tear, prayers, frustrating moments, arguments, prideful statements, humble submissions, apologies and forgiveness, honesty about life's pains, and a commitment to still remain.

I'm not always the problem, but, frankly, neither is he. Sometimes it's our past or our environment. There are times when it's work or school, confusion, or frustration with something & someone external. Yet home is where we lay our heads down. It's where we rest and let loose. It's where the dust settles as we try to find peace.

We have to know and understand this about our spouses, but most importantly we have to know it about ourselves. We have to give our spouses room to develop and breathe, but we also have to do the same thing for ourselves.

I've spoken to women that are frustrated with their husbands after they come home from work because they don't want to talk. They see their husbands get on technology and immediately take it as a sign of rejection. I've been in this place before.

Instead of realizing that he's just trying to cooldown from a long day at work, they think that something is wrong. That's the mind of a woman. We are always observing and interpreting because we want to be pleasing to our husbands. More than anything we want his affection and conversation. However, we have to learn how to communicate and be affectionate with our husbands in a way that is good for both parties.

I had to learn this over time. I had to come to a place where I knew that my husband wasn't frustrated with me; he just had a long day. There were times when he was frustrated with me, but I had to hear him out, think and pray about it, and then move on.

See, marriages have issues because there are two people involved, growing together. If there were never any issues, someone should be concerned because that would mean that stagnation is present.

Marriage makes you better and it makes him better too. Just look at the issues, chew up the meat and spit out the bones because some of it is just hogwash.

The heart of her husband trusts in her, and he will have no lack of gain. She does him good, and not harm, all the days of her life.

~Proverbs 31:11, 12

Looking at It

This morning as my husband was leaving the house; he kissed my youngest daughter and told her that she was beautiful. Then he leaned over and gave me a kiss. He looked at me and told me that I was beautiful too.

With all of my stinky morning breath, crusty eyes, and messed up hair, I said "Not right now, I'm not." In response to my awkward response to his affectionate and loving words, in which I had rejected myself and him, to a degree, he said… "Yes, you are! You're my wife."
Ok…wait! Did you get that?! Or did you miss it?!

He not only disregarded what I had said, but he also took it and turned it around by implying that because I am his wife, I am beautiful.

After he left, I read a devotional that illustrated how often we take the time to treat strangers and those that we don't really know, very well. Yet, we fail to treat ourselves and, sometimes, the ones we love, with that same kindness.

Normally I would have told a friend or someone who I didn't know, that they should not be so hard on themselves. Yet I was doing it.

So I took some time to think about this.

How does the way that I treat myself affect my relationships with others and more importantly, my relationship with God?

There are enough people and ads out there that tell me that I am not beautiful, too dark, my hair isn't straight enough. They say that I'm not smart enough, not tall enough, short enough, and bold enough. They say that I'm too feminine and too masculine. They tell me that I need to be more independent, but that I'm not dependent enough. You know…I smile too much, but don't smile enough. How about this one? I've been told that I am too organized, but not organized enough.

I don't know about you, but I don't think that I should listen to these voices. They don't seem too sure of the standard.

Then there is me…I am really hard on myself. I often hold myself to a very high standard. In many ways, I deal with perfectionism. We all know that I will never be perfect, in this life. In all actuality, I am aiming to be pleasing to God, but that ends up translating into trying too hard. I keep trying to do what is right in His eyes, but I hear the voices of people. I hear them rejecting my application. I hear them telling me that now is not the time and I'm not it.
My heart believes that He loves me and that I am accepted, but this head of mine…it's always fighting with my heart. Telling me that I am not special and most often, I am not wanted.

With all of this, I think I hear God saying that I am not good enough and He is not pleased…
But wait!!! That's not the truth.

He never said that. That's not even His character.

Much like my husband, He looks at me, in all of my mess. He has said "You are beautiful. You are mine." (see Isaiah 43:1)

He has said that his kindness would not depart from me; that he would have mercy on me, and that his covenant of peace would not be removed from me. (See Isaiah 54:10)

He has created me as I am supposed to be and he loves me. He will never leave me.

He has said the same thing to you.

Don't believe me?

Let's look at what the Bible says.

Psalm 139
    1. *O Lord, You have searched me and known me.*
    2. *You know my sitting down and my rising up; You understand my thought afar off.*
    3. *You comprehend my path and my lying down, And are acquainted with all my ways.*
    4. *For there is not a word on my tongue, But behold, O Lord, You know it altogether.*
    5. *You have hedged me behind and before, And laid Your hand upon me.*
    6. *Such knowledge is too wonderful for me; It is high, I cannot attain it.*
    7. *Where can I go from Your Spirit? Or where can I flee from Your presence?*
    8. *If I ascend into heaven, You are there; If I make my bed in hell, behold, You are there.*
    9. *If I take the wings of the morning, And dwell in the uttermost parts of the sea,*

10. Even there Your hand shall lead me, And Your right hand shall hold me.
11. If I say, "Surely the darkness shall fall on me," Even the night shall be light about me;
12. Indeed, the darkness shall not hide from You, But the night shines as the day; The darkness and the light are both alike to You.
13. For You formed my inward parts; You covered me in my mother's womb.
14. I will praise You, for I am fearfully and wonderfully made; Marvelous are Your works, And that my soul knows very well.
15. My frame was not hidden from You, When I was made in secret, And skillfully wrought in the lowest parts of the earth.
16. Your eyes saw my substance, being yet unformed. And in Your book they all were written, The days fashioned for me, When as yet there were none of them.
17. How precious also are Your thoughts to me, O God! How great is the sum of them!
18. If I should count them, they would be more in number than the sand; When I awake, I am still with You.
19. Oh, that You would slay the wicked, O God! Depart from me, therefore, you bloodthirsty men.
20. For they speak against You wickedly; Your enemies take Your name in vain.
21. Do I not hate them, O Lord, who hate You? And do I not loathe those who rise up against You?
22. I hate them with perfect hatred; I count them my enemies.
23. Search me, O God, and know my heart; Try me, and know my anxieties;
24. And see if there is any wicked way in me, And lead me in the way everlasting.

Are you able to see it? Have you realized why it is important not to be so hard on yourself? Meeting the expectations of the world is impossible because they don't know what they want. The world is tossed in every which way depending on the culture climate. However, our God is the same yesterday, today, and forever. The woman who He created you to be is the woman that He wants you to be. He gave you that hair, that skin, that smile, those teeth and all of your qualities. He has said that He would never leave us or forsake us. (see Joshua 1:9)

He has created us and in rejecting ourselves, we, in turn, reject Him. We are made in His image and with His love. He made us in a way that is magnificent and pleasing to Himself. All He wants is our love, obedience, and worship.

This in itself is another post, but let me leave you with this. If you don't love God with all of your heart, another god will sit on the throne of your heart and you will love it. If you don't obey God, you will submit to another authority and obey it. If you don't worship God, you will find something else to worship.

So, what am I getting at?

All of those other things, that will attempt to take the place of God and desire you, will never ever do what God has done for you. They have never taken the time to piece you together and they will never love you. They are not totally dedicated to seeing you at your best…only God can, has, and will do those things. He sent Jesus Christ to die for your sins and to wipe your slate clean.

Have you ever lied?

Have you ever stolen something?

Have you ever used the Lord's name in vain?

Have you ever looked at a man with lust in your heart?

Have you ever been jealous of what someone else had and wanted it?

Before Jesus, we were all liars, adulterers, and covetous thieves at heart. There was nothing left for us but to try hard and burn in eternal damnation away from God. Yet, Love paid the ultimate price and has now given us a chance to have life more abundantly here on earth…no more trying, just be who He has called you to be and walk with Him. You are also now able to have eternal life.

If you don't already know Jesus Christ as your Lord and Savior, please take a moment, in your heart to speak with the One true and living God. Accept His free gift of salvation, repent of your sins, and make Him the Lord of your life.

I can't promise you that there won't be days when you wake up feeling like I did. I can't promise you that you won't or that the world won't be so hard on you, but I can tell you that you don't have to be. I can tell you that God is there at the door and He wants to walk with you through your roughest times. This applies to you whether you have known the Lord for years or are just meeting Him.

> My prayer for you today is that you would have peace in Him.

For man was not made from woman, but woman from man. Neither was man created for woman, but woman for man.
1 Corinthians 11:8, 9

Know Your Place

Have you ever stopped for a moment to think about who you are and what that means? I know that I have.

Today's woman struggles with so much. Women of the past wanted the opportunities that we have today, but were banned from having them. Yet, we, as women of the 21st century, struggle with having our God-given roles and the open doors of opportunities that rest at our feet, for the taking. When we are given so many opportunities, without a clear understanding of who we are, we are liable to run in every direction, unknowingly, attempting to be someone that we are not. However, when we know who we are, we will only make the choices that we are called to make. We will step into the opportunities that fit our call.

Now you might think that I want to discuss with you, who you are as an individual. Instead, I want to take a look at who the Bible says that we are. What does God say about us? This is the perfect starting place. For it is here that we can begin to know the truth about who we are.

Let's take a look at what the Bible says about us as women.

The first appearance of a woman was in Genesis 2:22-24 where it says

And the Lord God made the rib (which He had taken from the man) into a woman. And He brought her to the man. And Adam said, this is now bone of my bones and flesh of my flesh.

She shall be called Woman because she was taken out of man. Therefore, shall a man leave his father and his mother, and shall cleave to his wife and they shall be one flesh.

In this first instance of the woman's appearing on the scene of humanity, she is made from an intricate part of the man, Adam. She is brought to the man, as a gift from God and He recognizes her as something special. It as if he is in awe. He says this is me. She is bone of my bones and flesh of my flesh. We are the same, but different; a compliment to one another. Thus, he rationalized within himself that a man should leave all that he has known to cleave to his wife because they are made for one another. They shall become one flesh.

There is a whole sector of women that find this portion of scripture degrading and humiliating. I am not talking to those women. Only God can change their minds. Instead I am talking to the woman who is a wife or wants to be one, someday.

This is the first time that we see a woman in the bible and, I think that, it is fantastic the way that she is presented, both to us and to Adam.
Let me show you how I see it.

God had created everything else in the world and Adam had the opportunity to look around at those amazing things. He looked up and saw the sky. He looked down and saw the grass beneath his feet. He looked around and saw the trees, named the animals, and even was able to take a look at his own reflection in the waters of Eden. He had even been given work to do. He was to tend to the garden of Eden, work and keep it.
Yet, in this world of having all that could satisfy him, he felt and was alone.

Stop...

Do you recognize something here? In this place of being provided with everything that He could ever need, this man felt and was alone. He had his needs met, but he had a want, and a longing that had not yet been fulfilled. Then this happened.

> *And the LORD God said, It is not good that the man should be alone.*
> *~Genesis 2:19*

The Lord knew that Adam would still feel alone, but He presented him with the animals of the field and the fowl of the air. He allowed Adam to name them, and he did. Yet, that need was still not met. When he was finished with work, he had no one to come home to; No one to cuddle with; No one with whom he could connect with in the most intimate way possible.

In this space in time, when woman had not yet appeared on the scene of creation, in the flesh, the earth was void of her presence. It was good, but Adam, its governor longed for something. He had no one that was suitable to come alongside him and help him in his doings. No one was available to complement him. No one was there to talk to him, as he worked; to encourage him, as he rested; to lavish her love upon him. At this point in creation, Adam had been so full, yet desired something more and only God knew what…excuse me, who that was. It was Eve, his woman.

When we read the Bible like this, there should be a dignity that rises up within us. We should not feel threatened by the presence of a man because we are what he wants, at the end of the day. Now, I do not dare to place us, as women, above God. For He alone can satisfy us all. I am only saying that when God was looking outside of Himself for the necessities in the earth that would bring Adam pleasure, He deemed it necessary to present Him with Eve. She was the conclusion, the big finale of His presentation. She was the "wow" factor.

Should we not take pride in being a man's wife? Yet, society has brought to us this idea that to be a man's wife and to be committed to him is a degrading thing. We are encouraged to leave the home and attempt to be <u>more than</u> his wife. We are served on a platter of world goods the idea that to "merely" be one's wife is to be less than because you should be more. Is being a wife not enough?

I want you to realize that you, as a wife, are not less than. You were created for this role, in life. Your part is very important upon the scene of humanity. Regardless of the mistakes that Eve, you, or I make, we were purposed to be here upon this planet in the position that we are in.

As my husband's wife, I do for him, what no other person upon this planet can do. I serve my husband's heart.

The heart of her husband trusts safely in her, so that he have no need of plunder. ~Proverbs 31:11

He knows that his heart is safe with me, regardless of the state that it is in at the time. I am able to see in to the depths of his being and to pray for his needs to our God. I am able to see his strengths and weaknesses. Yet, I do not expose him. I encourage him and love upon him. I offer him my respect because it is one of his deepest needs.

If I were to leave my place, I would leave him exposed to the world and the Jezebel like woman. She wishes to give him over to Satan, to dispose of him, and to leave him utterly confused & destroyed. For if she can destroy one man, she can destroy many. For she is being led by Satan to destroy the world, one man at a time.

We as women want to be needed and wanted, in this world. We want to fulfill a role that can never be fulfilled. We want to do what can never be done and on a grand scale. Have we never stopped to think for a moment that we are already doing that? When we are the women that God has called us to be, we are able to do something that no one else could ever do, hold the heart of one man. The man that God created. That is an honorable position and it is hard. Let's not down play this.

I asked God to let me change the world and it all started with the marriage of my husband. After him, I was blessed with four beautiful children. I don't need to look beyond this call to find something else. It is within this place of accepting my call that God has so graciously opened up other doors for me. He has shown me how and who else I can help, but I had to accept and walk in this first.

I challenge you to know and to identify your place. If you have been called as a wife or desire to be a wife, you have to long for the role of service. Not just to be loved and lavished upon, but to love and to hold your husband's heart. You have to be willing to abandon all that you know, according to the world, to learn the truth that God has set within you.

It is not foolish to trust the Lord and your husband. It is not foolish to pray that your marriage work and to work hard in it. Yes, the enemy and the world is busy pulling apart marriages, but that doesn't have to be your story. I am a living witness that this truth starts within us as women. We have to look at the world and the devil, square in the face and say "You cannot have my husband. He is mine." We have to tell the mountains of divorce, separation, chaos, and adultery to move out of our ways and out of our homes.

This takes bravery, consistency, patience, faithfulness, and trust in God to make it happen. There is a lot up against you, but if you know your place, nothing can take it away from you. You have to pray consistently. You have to fill yourself with the word of God. You have to be willing to turn away from the worldly things, the television shows, the wrong books, the wrong people & relationships. You know the ones that I am talking about. I live in today's society, as well, and this is a battle that has to be fought on a daily basis.

We are in a war. It is a war for our souls and a war for the hearts of men. God has placed us, a band of women in this position because no one else can do it. No one else will love God and His man enough to take a stand and fight the great fight of faith. To protect and serve the heart of man takes a <u>woman.</u>

Will you? Will you get focused enough to really know and take your place?

and the two shall become one flesh.' So they are no longer two but one flesh.
~Mark 10:8

Is Your Husband Flawed

When I first married my husband, I was convinced that he was a great guy. I knew that he would always love me and show me that he cared.

As we moved into our second, third, fourth, and even fifth year of being married, I could see his flaws more than I could see them originally. I considered how I thought he had changed and was determined to help him remember the qualities that he had possessed before, which qualified him for the "great guy" category.

What I did not know was that he had always been a flawed individual, but because of the love, passion, and desire that I had for him, I could not see them.

When we were dating, my husband would show up early for our dates. He would ring the door bell and then patiently wait for me, on the couch or in the car. When we arrived to our destination, we were always early.
Later on in our marriage, he would get ready and promptly remind me of my need to speed up, as I got dressed. He wanted us to arrive early to our destination, but I was taking my time getting dressed.

Before marriage…not a flaw….

After marriage…flaw…

Over the years, I had tried to change various aspects of who he was, but learned that it was more difficult to change him, than it was to change something in myself.

What I mean is that I started to ask myself why certain aspects of his personality seemed to be flaws to me now, when they were not flaws to me before…

He had always been very punctual…nothing had changed about him.

Had I been unaware of the changes that had occurred in my own personality over the years? The more I asked this question, the deeper I dug into the root of my issue. The more I dug, the more I prayed. The more I prayed, the more God began to show me…myself.

He helped me to see that I wasn't perfect, but He never considered me so flawed that I could not be loved. He showed me that He had actually given me time, as He would continue to in the future, to get past certain struggles and be the woman that he created me to be. He showed me that there were various aspects of myself that would need to be changed before He would consider me mature. Yet that never changed how He saw me. It never changed the fact that He considered me precious and lovable.

Learning to see myself through God's eyes, helped me to see my husband in the same way. I began to accept who he was and his "flaws" became characteristics that I cherished. Our differences came to be the strengths of our marriage, when previously, I had considered them weaknesses.

Today, I am a more punctual person. Although I still struggle with consistency, my husband's ability to remain consistent will definitely rub off on me, I'm sure. I consider that my perspective is often times what needs to be changes, not my husband. God will and does work on him, but my job is to allow Him to work on me.

I love my husband more and more each day. I cherish the ways that he sharpens me like iron, even when it's not comfortable at the moment. When I look back on it all, I am thankful.

If you were to ask me if my husband is flawed, I would humbly say, "Yes, he is, but so am I. We are both human." Can you relate to what I have said here? Do you find it easier to identify the "flaws" of your spouse that it is to identify your own flaws? How can you change your perspective and actions to make the weaknesses of your marriage the strength of your marriage?

*Know this, my beloved brothers: let
every person be quick to hear, slow to speak,
slow to anger;*

James 1:19

Communication with your Husband

The other night, I was in a marriage coaching session with a couple. After we had finished, I sat and thought about the communication between these two spouses. I gradually began to think about my communications with my husband over the past 13 1/2 years.

I realized that many times couples underestimate the effectiveness of loving, open-hearted communication. When we were in our first two years of marriage, I remember thinking that good couples in healthy marriages did not argue. Now that I have been married to my high school sweetheart for more than a decade, I have come to realize that some of the best couples indeed argue. They are just careful about how they do it.

Many times in life, we try to avoid some of the hardest situations. When we are in the fire, we run away, refusing to get burned. What we fail to realize is that somethings require fire in order to be refined, like gold. That is how our lives are.

We spend a lot of time around people who want to tickle our ears. They don't want to ruffle our feathers because they are afraid that challenging our perspectives will jeopardize the relationship that they have with us. Yet, without challenges, we cannot become better individuals or live our best lives for Christ. Without challenges, we are stuck in our same ol' ways, smiling, but never better. However, marriage is not one of those relationships, nor should it be.

In a marriage each partner, by default, should make the other better.

Think about it. This is the person that lives with you and sees you at you best…and worst. He knows when you are giving something your all and when you are doing it half way. He can see when you are walking in love and walking in anger. To be even more precise, he can see what you cannot see about yourself and speak truth to you about it, in love.

I know, it doesn't always feel like he is speaking in love, but what if you adjusted your hearing. Do you think that you could turn down your detection of pessimism, resentment, and anger long enough to detect the love that he has in his heart for you? Do his words challenge you and call you out of fear? Does he confirm what God has already spoken into your heart about the changes that you need to make to be your best?

I have found that over the course of my marriage, communication with my husband has not always been easy, but more times than not, it has been very beneficial. I have had to make a choice to remain accountable, open-hearted, and humble towards him, so that he could lead me.

Yes, I said that my husband leads me. When I have prayed for direction and I'm looking for someone to speak into my life, God will often use my husband to say some of the toughest things to me. Because his eyes are watching me each day, I have also been held accountable.

In trusting our husbands with our hearts, we leave room for God to speak to us through them. He is able to validate us through the one human relationship that will be most fulfilling on this earth.

Husbands, love your wives, just as Christ also loved the church and gave Himself for her, that He might sanctify and cleanse her with the washing of water by the word, that He

might present her to Himself a glorious church, not having spot or wrinkle or any such thing, but that she should be holy and without blemish. So husbands ought to love their own wives as their own bodies; he who loves his wife loves himself. For no one ever hated his own flesh, but nourishes and cherishes it, just as the Lord does the church. For we are members of His body, of His flesh and of His bones. "For this reason a man shall leave his father and mother and be joined to his wife, and the two shall become one flesh." This is a great mystery, but I speak concerning Christ and the church. Nevertheless let each one of you in particular so love his own wife as himself, and let the wife see that she respects her husband.
~Ephesians 5:22-33

Today, I want to encourage you to consider the communication that you have with your husband. Don't think that it always has to sound or look a certain way in order for it to be effective. It should not be abusive, but it doesn't have to be pretty either. It needs to be what God knows is best for you in your life and in your marriage. Your husband loves you and servers God in helping you though this process of sanctification and cleansing that God is so mercifully taking you through. See the fire and the flame as methods used to make you better. Never stop talking to, texting, emailing, winking, or smiling at your husband. Leave the lines of communication open and know that in a loving relationship, iron sharpens iron.

*She does him good and not evil
All the days of her life.
~Proverbs 31:12*

Called to Duty & to Change

A few years ago, when we had been married for eight years, I was pregnant with our third child. I had been used to my husband being home with us. At this time he had been notified by his unit that he would have to leave home for 3-4 months at a time every 3-4 months.

When this happened, I had no idea what to expect. I had two little children and was pregnant. I wanted my husband home with me, but I had to understand what his career required. I wasn't sure what my life would be like in the next few months, but I trusted God.

I grew up in my home as an only child, so I knew what it was like to be alone, but I had grown accustomed to having my husband with me as my companion. At night we would have dinner together, walk the dog, read to our boys, and kiss one another goodnight. I told myself that I would have to find a new normal, but I was really emotional and pregnant.

My third pregnancy was a hard one. I was plagued with nausea that lasted for weeks. I wasn't sure what to do, so I started reading my Bible more and more. It was something that I had done during our earlier years of marriage, when I was stressed. At this time in my life, I found great peace in reading the Word of God.

Although I wasn't sure what to expect at the beginning of this time, when my husband would leave, by the end of his time away, I had come to cherish the times that I had with God.

I missed my husband dearly, but I loved my time with God. I'm sure my husband also recognized the changes that had occurred in me due staying in the Word.

When he returned home, I was a different woman. I was less emotional, more focused, and filled with more joy. I have come to believe that there will be times, during my husband's career, when God will pull him away and take the opportunity to make me better. During these times, He changes me and touches an area of my life that I didn't even know needed to be changed.

For this very reason, my mind has changed about my husband leaving. I don't look forward to it. I still miss him dearly, but I have come to expect that I will be very different when he returns because God wants to do something in me.

I believe that now I can honestly say my husband is called to duty and I am called to change.

Have you ever had a similar experience when it comes to your husband leaving? What joy have you found in the experience, if any?

If you enjoyed reading this post, please consider subscribing to my email list. I offer weekly encouragement and exclusive monthly content.

But the fruit of the Spirit is love, joy, peace, longsuffering, kindness, goodness, faithfulness, gentleness, self-control. Against such there is no law.

~Galatians 5:22, 23

Taking Charge of Your Emotions in Your Marriage

When I was first married, I was an emotional mess. I had just finished graduating from high school, leaving my mother's house, coming back from military training, and I was still dealing with issues of my past. Although I believed in God, I had not really developed a relationship with Him, so my faith was founded in religion and not in my relationship with Him.

When I say that I was an emotional mess, I mean I had been dealing with my emotions from childhood. I held a lot in and didn't say how I was feeling when I was upset, frustrated, or disappointed. I attempted to wear a straight face to mask my saddening emotions, but that would quickly fail, as I spent a lot of time crying. Looking back on it, I know that some of these feelings came from feeling unheard and rejected.

So, I was 19, married, in the army, expecting our first child, and dealing with a lot of adult issues that I had no idea how to handle. I brought the same pattern of holding in my emotions until they exploded, into my marriage. I would keep everything that my husband was doing or saying, that bothered me, bottled up inside. Then when I couldn't hold it in anymore, I would blow up. I would get so upset with him and unload on him, that he could not keep track of all my complaints. If I am to be honest, some of them were big, but others were small and even minute.

My problem was that I was holding on to too many things and I wasn't in right relationship with God, so I didn't know how to give him the issues and concerns that were bothering me. If I could be honest with you, during that first year of my marriage, I was so upset with God that I didn't what to have anything to do with Him. I had experienced a lot and wondered why He would allow me to go through it all, so I shunned Him.

I didn't go to church or want to hear about church. I didn't want to talk about God or read the Bible. I tried going to the club, drinking, and fixing my own problems. By the end of my 19th year on this earth, I was so distraught that I wanted to give up.

…but God didn't leave me there. He had my mother invite me to church to sell Mary Kay during an event and I went. I had decided that I would leave prior to the service beginning, but God had other plans.

Right when the service was about to start, I packed up my items and attempted to run out the door. I had folded up my table and was taking out my last box, when the music hit me and I could not move. I was stopped as I sensed the presence of God providing for me what I had not experienced in some time, comfort. This story is an entire chapter or book in itself, so I want to tell you that God completely changed my life in one moment.

He made His presence so real to me that I could no longer deny or reject Him. If I did, I would be turning from the best relationship I would have ever known. This was the point that began to change me, but it would take some years to become visible.

As I was relying on God, I was confused about how to handle my emotions, my relationship, my concerns, and so much more. When something would happen, I would be so frustrated that one event had the capacity to ruin my entire day. I had no control over my emotions, at all.

I would hear people talk about the fruit of the Spirit, but I had no idea how it applied to my life. Then I started to really study and follow the word of God. As I began to live it, I saw that God was making His qualities manifest in my life.

After about 6 years of walking with God in a fully committed relationship to Him, I began to teach the fourth grade girls at my church. In preparation for the year, I had to study the fruit of the Spirit and find ways of illustrating them at work in life. This experience blew my mind.

I began to see that there were complete sections in time, when God was working on me in regards to the fruit. There was a year or so when He worked on me with love. Another few months to a year where showed me how to have joy. He taught me how to choose peace. I begin to experience long suffering because I had to endure the trials of life and continue to be faithful. This pattern continued until my character had been shaped by the characteristics that please God most. My life began to produce fruit and I am continually, to this day, being given new lessons of how to live and walk in the fruit of the Spirit.

Ok…so I know that you might be thinking, "Makeda, what does this have to do with handling my emotions in my marriage?" Well, I'm glad that you asked because I'm going to tell you.

The world gives us all of these tools and techniques to try to maintain our composure when we are upset, but if there is no spiritual foundation to the principles, they are ineffective in actually shaping and changing us.

When we choose the fruit of the Spirit, we are opting into trusting God to help us, by the Holy Spirit to walk upright and to have control over our reactions to the physical world, through spiritual application and methods over our natural, fleshly, human, and carnal emotions. We are choosing to align our entire being with the Spirit of God, which produces fruit because we are not walking according to the flesh.

Here's what I mean. Let's say that my husband is upset with me for a reason that I don't understand, yet. He decided that he doesn't want to talk to me right now because he is upset, but it confuses me because I have no idea what's going on. He leaves the house for work, telling me to have a good day, because we do not depart from one another without saying goodbye and wishing the other well, but never telling me what's wrong. There are two ways that this could go.

The first is that I could do what I used to do when I didn't give it over to God or talk to Him about it. I'd fret and worry for hours on end trying to figure out what I had done and why he was so upset with me. I would take him not talking to me as rejection, of me his wife and as a woman. I would conclude that he did not believe that I was worthy of his time or his words. These thoughts would cause me to feel overwhelmed and emotional. Quickly, rejection would appear and control my entire day. I could take care of my children, but cleaning and focusing on projects for school became hard at this time because I was preoccupied by emotions. None of my perceived thoughts about what my husband was thinking was accurate. He loved me and valued me. He just didn't want to talk.

Doing this is tiring. You never know how you are going to feel, when someone does or says something that you do don't like. You live at the whim of other people because the drop of a dime frustrates you, or at least it did me.

Still, there is a better way, the second option. I could see that that something is bothering my husband. Say "good morning" and continue to go conduct my daily activities. Then I could take a moment to tell God that something is bothering him and ask Him to reveal it to me. Once my husband leaves, saying "goodbye," I simply wish him well and sincerely, without any other concerns, tell him to have a good day.

This requires patients and trust. When I do this, I have to know that God heard me, when I submitted my concern to Him. I have to believe that He is going to take care of my husband and I because the world is not over when someone is upset. From there, I have to proceed with interacting in my relationship with God, so that my focus is not on my husband, but on the Lord.

By this time, a word has come up in my spirit and I hear something, "choose peace." Thinking about this further, I ask the Lord to help me understand. I'm taking care of my children and cleaning as I'm talking to the Lord, but I am seeking Him because I heard His voice through my conscious. I ask Him to help me to choose peace and the word again arises in my heart. "the peace of God that surpasses all understanding…Focus on the Lord."

Let me stop for a moment. I used to ask and wonder how to know that something was from the Lord. Nana told me that whenever you hear the scripture or positive words come to your mind, that it is instruction from God. When you hear something like that, you are supposed to do it or say it. I praise God for her. She helped me to understand, when I had no way of comprehending the truth.

Now back to the second option. After choosing to focus on the Lord, I have to choose to listen and obey. I have to choose to allow my concerns to subside and fade away, not because I am pretending that they didn't happen, but because I gave them to God. I have to trust Him with my heart and my concerns. So, I think on things that are lovey, or of good report, of virtue...something praiseworthy. I turn on the music and listen to songs that are uplifting and spiritual. Doing this allows me to focus on something beyond my emotions and my husband's frustration. While there will be time to focus on him, now is not THE time. I have to take care of my children and perform my obligations.

Taking this second step over time begins to build in me character for living in peace. It trains my mind and emotions to understand that the carnal side of me does not have rule and reign over who I am and how I function. I give control over to my spirit that is in line with the Holy Spirit within me, and I live in the goodness and peace of God.

When you live like this, nothing can steal your joy. Things will try. Let me say that again...things will try, but you always have to refocus on the things of the Lord. You always have to give over your concerns and cares to Him, knowing that things will be fine.

By the end of the day, my husband would come home and tell me what was bothering him. Normally it would be something that I could easily fix or need to pray for help with, but it's not a life changing concern. We go on with our lives and trust God to continue to make our marriage grow. We love each other so much, but emotional damage of the past has tried to break us. I have had to learn not to give the enemy of my marriage a foothold in the door of my marriage, though my emotions. When other things come up, I have to pray and speak against it, trust God and move on.

Do you struggle with this? How do you handle your emotional times in your marriage? Does your husband get the worst part of who you are when you are emotional or are you able to walk in the Spirit?

A Pray for Your Marriage

There are times when you have to put your knees to the floor and seek the one that is more than able to do the impossible for and on behalf of you and your husband. This is a prayer that you can pray for your marriage.

Father God, I come to you, as humbly as I know how, thanking you for your lovingkindness and tender mercies. Thank you for life health and strength. Thank you for relationship and marriage. Father, I ask you to first and for most, forgive me of all sins that I have committed both knowingly and unknowingly. Show me the ways that I can be better for you, for myself, and for my husband. I surrender myself to you and trust that you will not allow me to be harmed. Lord, I lay before you now the cares of my marriage. I lay my husband's heart before you and ask you to have your way. Help us to continually grow together in you, as we become one. Draw us closer to one another and to Yourself. Bless our intimacy, in the natural, emotional, and in the spiritual areas. Tear down the walls that we have erected to protect ourselves against hurt, so that the other can truly get close to the other's heart. Place a hedge of protection around us and all that is ours. Let no one and nothing come between us. I take authority, right now, over every satanic attack that has been plotted, planned, and set in motion against my marriage. I rebuke the evil that has come up against us and cancel all evil plans, in the might name of Jesus. Lord, I rebuke confusion because you are not the God of confusion. I rebuke divorce because you hate divorce. I rebuke the spirit of fornication, masturbation, adultery, pride, hatred, and separation from my marriage in the name of Jesus. Remove all of those that will attempt to separate or come between us and to hinder or destroy our relationship with you. As I tell all of those things to go, I invite You into our secret places. Bless us and keep us, Lord. Help my husband to love me and me to respect him. Teach us to submit to your will and to fight for our marriage. Allow us to help others, as you have helped us. Let Your purpose and will for our marriage be done in the name of Jesus. Lord as we lean on you, drawing close to one another and to You, please allow us to feel your presence and experience your peace and prosperity in our marriage. Strengthen every area of our marriage because I give it to You and You have said in Your word that if I place my hope and trust in You, I would not be put to shame. You said that You would never leave us or forsake us, Lord, so I look to this relationship being a blessing to both my life and my husband's life. In the mighty name of Jesus, I thank you Lord and I pray. ~Amen

I recommend that you pray this prayer, out loud, frequently. If you find yourself in a rough spot, pray it daily. If you don't, pray it daily. Either way, I recommend that you set your alarm on your phone and pray for your marriage on a daily basis. If you don't, the enemy will attempt to find loopholes to attack both you and your husband.

Being a Mother

*"Hear, my son, your father's instruction
and do not forsake your mother's teaching;
Indeed, they are a graceful wreath to your
head and ornaments to your neck."*
~Proverbs 1:8-9

Mother...

If you carry this title, then you know that you have been blessed by the Lord, with a gift that can only come from heaven.

I remember when I would pray and ask the Lord if I could be a part of changing the world. His answer to me was the birth of my four beautiful babies. They each have different gifting's, talents, and callings upon their lives. They each have specific ways in which they will touch the world, in some capacity.

Mother is a title that I have been honored to hold. With each day, I have the opportunity to pour into their lives in ways that no one else can. For they only have one mother.

The thing about being a mother is that I don't only think about my children, but I think about children from all over. My heart breaks for the child that lost her mother, less than a year ago. I yearn to help the child that is left alone because his mother has to work. I even desire to befriend the mother that is in need of a loving relationship with another mother.

Yet, I realize that there is something imperative that each mother do, if she is to make her mark upon her children, as deemed by the Lord. She is to first seek the Lord through prayer about all that she is and ever will be.

As mothers, we are far from perfect, but God has placed something very important within us that our children need. We may not know what it is, but He does.

As you read this, I challenge you to pray, be changed by God, and give your children your best. Don't be afraid to apologize when you are wrong, hug them and love them beyond yourself, see and recognize their needs. Tell them how valuable and important they are.

I challenge you because the world wants them lonely and motherless. It wants them broken and rejected. It wants them longing for…a mother.

If my mother did not do anything else, she showed me and told me of my value and worth. Her actions implied that I was important and the way that she spent her time, displayed that I was worth it.

If we seek the Lord and allow Him to work by His Holy Spirit, through us, there will never be a void available for the world to fill…at least not a motherless void.

I'll be praying for you in your Motherhood.

Her children rise up and call her blessed;

Her husband also, and he praises her:

Proverbs 31:28

The Love of a Mother

I have been a mother now for 15 years. I have four children and I have often heard people say, "Wow! You have four children. I don't know how you do it. How do you do it?"

When I hear them say this I realize that they are only asking because the world has trained our minds to believe that four children is a lot. It's really not a lot though.

Each of my grandparents had two to four children. Before that my great grandparents had four to six children. Prior to that my maternal grandparents had 17 children. They had 13 of their own children and raised 4 of a family member's children.

They taught their children to care for and support one another. They showed them how to live and they led them in the ways of the Lord.

Our society today teaches us that an abundance of family is a curse, when in reality, it's a blessing.

God blesses us with children. He gives them to us, straight out of heaven. Yes, I know the biology behind it, but the life sustaining power comes from God.

As you raise your children, you have to keep this in mind. You also have to remember that God has equipped you as a mother to raise your children. The situations that arise will stretch you, but the stretching will make you a better mother.

You have to love your children out of a godly type of unconditional love. You can't love them out of your pain or teach them out of your frustration. You have to deal with yourself before you can attempt to deal with your children.

So many people say to their children what their parents said to them. These are the things that they hated growing up, but they still say them. They break down the self-esteem of their children and never give them a chance of being functionally high esteemed, socially connected, spiritually astute individuals.

It's sad. So many children leave home at 18 broken. They never want to look back, but they do because…family is back there. They hear things like, "you don't get to choose your family members" and despise being raised in the household that they were brought up in. They end up having mommy and daddy issues all because parents didn't do the work on themselves to make sure that they were not emotionally bruising their children.

Sure, you might get loud sometimes, but you aren't screaming at the top of your lungs. You aren't screaming obscenities at your children. You aren't dealing with them out of anger from your past.

No!

You are taking the time with God and allowing Him to help you process your own childhood and current emotions, so that you can be a good mother to your own children.

My children often times hear me, early in the morning, as they are getting ready for school, getting on each other's nerves, saying "Lord help me with my children today, Father. I need to know what to say and do."

They have literally looked at each other and told one another to chill out because mom is praying about what to do.

This is the power of being a godly mother.

I don't always have it under control, but who does. I do have to have myself under control though.

I really have to walk in the fruit of the Spirit.

> *But the fruit of the Spirit is love, joy, peace, forbearance, kindness, goodness, faithfulness, gentleness and self-control.*
> *~Galatians 5:22, 23*

I have to be willing to listen to the Holy Spirit as I take care of my four children that outnumber me and how many hands I have. Hmmph...

I didn't understand this before I had children. I thought that it took a certain amount of skill, but what it really takes is patience and a heart that's willing to seek God for the benefit of a person that can't do it for themselves.

We have to be willing to ask God to create in us a clean heart and to renew a right spirit in us on a daily basis because our children need us.

You can't take care of someone else, if you're broken into pieces.

So before you throw up your hands and say that you aren't enough because you aren't a super mom like ____, consider that she isn't either. Take your concerns to the Lord and realize that none of us are perfect. That's what helps our children grow.

They watch our lives and learn. When they see us becoming better people, they learn that there is always potential for growth.

When they see families that are upset come together for dinner, they learn the healthy relationships endure conflict and continue to love one another amiss the emotions.

Show your children how to love and do this God's way.

Love is patient, love is kind. It does not envy, it does not boast, it is not proud.

1 Corinthians 13:4

The Love of a Child

When I first became a mother I never knew what it would be like. I spent a lot of time thinking and dreaming, but I didn't know that my children would bring such joy into my life. I used to think of holding them and changing their diapers, but I didn't expect the things that they would add to my life.

Today, I can see some of what they add and how they bless me. I have a 13 year old that makes me laugh. He challenges me in ways that make me proud to say that I am his mother. Often times he comes to me and tells me new things that he has learned about the earth, animals, books, and our environment. Still the challenges that we face together of puberty, chores, and integrity are all just beginning, as he grows into a young man.

In a few weeks, my 8 year old will be nine. This young man is my affectionate little guy. Just the other day, after I had gone grocery shopping and picking up a few things for him, he continually wrapped his arms around me to show his appreciation. Over and over again, he thanked me and although I had not done anything out of the ordinary, I felt so special and honored by the amount of gratitude he had shown me. He tells me stories of things and shows me pictures of things that he has imagined. As he matures, I am excited to see the type of young man he will become.

My oldest daughter, but third child, is a lot like me. She is 6 years old loves to sing, dance, write, talk, read and is very creative. Every day, I am amazed by her love for life. She offers me great challenges as she is inquisitive about the reasons for decisions that we make in our home. Yet, I never tire of her intelligence. I am proud to be her mother. I look forward to being there for her as she grows in to a beautiful young lady. She says that she aspires to be like me, which is an honor, but also a reason why I strive to be they godly woman that God would be proud of. I hope that one day, I will see that she has surpassed me in character and wisdom. I look forward to seeing her as a godly young woman who has made good choices for her life.

My youngest and last child is a beautiful little girl. She is two years and as I type keeps pretending to put lotion on my hands. I have noticed that she has learned very quickly they ways of a young lady. She spends a lot of time with me, since she is the only one home with me during the day. She enjoys singing, reading, pretending to do the things she sees me do. I hope that she always enjoys life as much as she does now.

Together, these four beautiful children brighten up my life. They put smiles on my face. I remember praying and telling God that I wanted to change the world. I wanted to make a difference. I realize that He has given me four children to love and who love me. This is my opportunity to change the world. I pour all that I can into them and pray that the seeds that I plant will take root and one day my children will produce great fruit.

I cannot express my love enough for them, but I know that their loves changes me. They show me such great love that reminds me of the love of God. I know that one day, they will grow up and will look at my life. Although I am not perfect, I hope they understand my choices and my responses to things that have happened in our lives. Knowing that our relationships will one day change, as they change, but I hope that we will be able to grow together in love and mature in our relationships together.

This, love that my children have for me, reminds me of the love that I have for my parents. Although our relationships have changed and will continue to do so as long as we live, I love them. I try my best to understand the choices that they make and the hardships that they have faced. Yet, I love them still the same. I hope that my mother always feels that I have honored her and knows that I love her. I also hope that my father knows that I have cherished his wisdom and have always tried to respect him. I hope he knows that I love him as well.

The love between parent and child is one that can change the lives of both recipients. I will forever be changed by the blessings that God has chosen to give me through my children.

I will instruct thee and teach thee in the way which thou shalt go: I will guide thee with mine eye.

~Psalm 32:8

What to Expect When...

Wow! What a day?! It was an action packed adventure. There were ups and downs. I had me a couple ins and outs. As I sat down tonight, with all of the kids asleep, I wondered if there is a seminar, book, DVD, or cd that could help us when it comes to raising our kids. I remember that book "What to expect when you're expecting," or even "What to expect during the first year."

Those are great books, but there should be one called "What to expect when parenting...period."

Let me tell you, I need a copy! It should say something like...

Expect to be challenged
Expect ups and downs
Expect messy clothes and poopy diapers
Expect dirty faces and possible poopy hands
Expect booger eating
Most of all expect the unexpected...
Man, what is a mom to do?

I just know that there should have been a class in high school that would give women a realistic view on raising children older than one years old. Now, I love my children, I am just tired. I need some sleep and honestly after a day like the one I had...I should be tired. I must say, I am learning what to expect from my children. Maybe I should write the book...What to expect when parenting...PERIOD!!!

Children are a gift from the Lord;

they are a reward from him.

Psalm 127:3

What to do?

Being a mom is a big task.

It's a full time job. It's not just about the cleaning, cooking, and taking the kids to school. There are a lot of decisions that moms have to make. There are big questions like, "can I pack my lunch for school tomorrow," "where are my Elmo socks," and not to mention the big one, "can I have a snack?" These questions could plague the everyday individual and drive them up the wall, but to a mother, it's an everyday occurrence.

Did I mention that with all that a mother has to do, she has to schedule herself a shower? At least this mother over here does. That's funny, huh?! I guess you would think so. I do too.

Nana has always told me to make sure that I was well rested. When my children were babies and even as I currently have a toddler, she has told me to sleep when they are sleeping. She has always reminded me that I cannot push past my human capacity to be a mom, but I'm not supposed to. She told me that I won't know all of the answers, but as I seek God, I would need no man to teach me because God would equip me as a mother. Wisdom would come because it was sent by God, but she always encouraged me to trust who God created me to be.

Yep, but that's that life of a mom. Really, there are things that moms have to think about that others don't. I have to ask myself almost every day how much do we have planned to do and how much of it are we really going to get done. I have to look at my kids and make sure that they aren't getting worn out from all of the running, doing, and visiting. I even have to make sure that they aren't suffocated by being in the house too much.

That seems like a lot, but I thank God that He helps me along the way. I mean, without Him, I don't think I would make it and I probably wouldn't be too good of a mom either. I'm not exaggerating. This job is a hard one and I tip my hat off to those mothers who have to work outside of the home and inside of the home. Thank God for the grace that He gives us to be who He has called us to be.

So tonight I have had to make an executive decision…all events must stop. My son passed out doing his homework and we had somewhere to go, but I think it will be alright if we don't go, this time.

Splendor and majesty are before him; strength and joy are in his place.
1 Chronicles 16:27

Renegade Bus Driver

Renegade- an individual who rejects lawful or conventional behavior.

Conventional behavior of a bus driver- pick up kids. Its 6:40am and I have my keys in my hand. I'm telling my oldest son to go the car and get his jacket. As he walks out the door, he sees his bus flying by the house.

Now his bus was supposed to be at the bus stop at 6:45am, but all at once she had made her way past six different stops. Before I could yell out anything, my son is running down the street after the bus. He finally stops and turns around disappointed. I'm not sure if it was because the bus didn't slow down or because he really thought that he was going to be able to catch it. At the speed she was going, she drove all the way around our neighborhood which is about 13 streets in less than six minutes. So I jumped in my car, shoes off, and drove my son to the bus.

I cut through a couple of streets to get to the other side of the neighborhood. When I got there I wasn't surprised to see other parents who had jumped in the car with their kids, to take them to the bus. There also came a long line of kids running to the bus. I asked a parent who was standing by the bus to let the driver know that there were kids around the neighborhood waiting to be picked up. She came back saying that the bus driver was looking at her like she was crazy. As I drove off I asked the driver to put her window down and she had a look on her face like I know. Did she know that there were many parents driving through the neighborhood trying to find that bus?

It was a sight to see. All I could think was renegade bus driver. Yes she is new, but she has made these stops before. My son told me that she does this in other neighborhoods as well. I guess she says, "You know what, I'm not picking them up. I know I'm early, but if they aren't out here, their getting left." I wonder what her plan was. Did she plan on showing up at the school with 70% of the students on her bus missing? I wonder what the administrators would have said…"You didn't feel like picking them up this morning, huh? It's ok. I've been there before"… I think not!

Too funny! Well in a, "I hope that never happens again, kind of way." It could have been frustration, but it wasn't. It made for a good laugh this morning. And I wish I had my camera to catch my son running down the block, chasing after the renegade bus driver.

And his mother used to make for him a little robe and take it to him each year when she went up with her husband to offer the yearly sacrifice.
1 Samuel 2:19

On Parenting

Wow!!!

Was that Wednesday? I had my share of ups and downs yesterday. I had moments when everything went well and others where they just didn't. But that's how life is, right?!

Each and every day…in every season of our lives we are faced with new challenges. We have to make new decisions. We have to decide to either commit or not to commit to a task, function, or a role.

I find that these are the times when I begin to reevaluate my priorities. I look at my progress. Am I consistent in what I do? Am I holding myself accountable or do I have someone in my life that can do it for me when I can't?

Yet, parenting is one of those things where you never know what trials or tests we are going to face. Parenting tests our ability and our inabilities. It is one of the many roles in life that test or check our character. Parenting proves if we are who we say we are…who we hope to be…or who we said we would never be…

It is in this, that we have to stand strong in the promises of God…cast all of our cares upon Him…for He cares for us…

When I need wisdom…I ask…He supplies…

Parenting causes me to say *"Lord, help me to push when I need to push, but not pass the limit that you have set...that is needed...Help me to hold on when I should and to let go when I need to...Help me Lord to raise them right...pleasing in Your sight. For you gave them to me...Let me stand up for them and with them...when I should against their will to do wrong...to quit, to not try...help me to teach them resilience and accountability. Help me to show them the way that you have shown me..."*

This is my hearts prayer...for me...for my husband...for my children...my grandchildren...

I even pray this for you...that you would be encouraged and strengthened to influence and assist a young person in their growth and maturity. When you feel like giving up, that God would equip you with the strength to continue to go on and to see the task all the way through...

That was Wednesday...over that hump...

Now, this is Thursday...

Train up a child in the way he should go,

And when he is old he will not depart from it.

Proverbs 22:6

Bringing Up Children

Have you ever thought about what it takes to bring up children? How are parents supposed to help children become responsible educated adults? Have you ever wondered what kind of time and effort it would require or the amount of commitment that it would take?

The truth is that not too many people do. Many people may even say, "There's nothing to it, but to do it. Right?!"

WRONG!!!

That's right! I used all capital letters and three exclamation points. I want you to think about this. There is more to it than just doing it.

Train up a child in the way he should go: and when he is old, he will not depart from it. ~Proverbs 22:6

Train up a child. Think about training and all that goes into it on the part of the trainer and the trainee. That means that a lot of hard work, preparation, educating, correcting, and patience will be needed. Now, that is a lot to be required of parents, but there is more that will be needed. Parents have to be willing to make choices and to stand behind them. They have to teach their children right from wrong and be willing to discipline them when they are wrong. With all of that, there is more…

The world will come up against everything that a parent attempts to instill in a child. Here are a few examples of what parents will encounter:

Parent: "Wear your coat."
Child: "I don't want to wear my coat. Bobby, Susan, and Jane don't have their coats on."
Parent: "I'm not their mother.
At this point the parent will have to decide what to do. Will the parent give in or stand behind the decision that was originally made.
Parent: "We don't use that type of language!"
Child: "Why not? I heard it on t.v…"
Parent: "Because it's wrong and foul."
Child: "But Jane talks like that all the time and her mother doesn't say anything."

The parent has to decide how to handle the situation.

Parents have to talk to their children about drinking, drugs, sex, friendships, faith, morals, and so much more. It is our responsibility to teach and train our children. When they leave our homes, they are supposed to be responsible, educated, morally good, adults. If you are a Christian, like I am, then our children should also leave our homes filled with faith, knowing how to pray, and trust God in all situations. They should not be afraid to make hard choices. In fact, they should expect to and realize that making those choices will change the lives of those around them.

Training up children is not easy, but it is an honorable job. What the world wants for my children is not what is important to us. Instead we focus in on what God wants for them. As a mother, I teach them to be children that will one day grow into individuals of integrity who, by their lives, will change the world around them, for the better.

So the next time you are confronted with making a hard decision as a parent, know that you are fully equipped to do so. The decisions that you make for your children will determine who they become and who they will be when you are long gone. It is a parent's job to bring up their children…

In righteousness you shall be established; you shall be far from oppression, for you shall not fear; and from terror, for it shall not come near you.
Isaiah 54:14

Am I Enough

I'm not sure if I'm the only mom that thinks this way, but with my fourth baby on the way, I find that I keep asking myself…"Am I enough?"

It's not that I feel like a bad mother or anything, but there are times when I wonder if I am fully equipped to raise my four children. I thank God that I am not doing it alone. I have my wonderful husband walking alongside me as we bring up these four children.

I think part of my thinking this morning comes from watching too much Law and Order yesterday. It's been a while since I've seen a show, but yesterday there was some sort of marathon on. Since I wasn't feeling very well, I laid in my bed and watched the T.V.

With each episode, came another devastating situation. With some I wondered what could be done, but with others I asked…how could they? I'm not sure how many I watched, but the various topics got me thinking about life and the consequences of wrong doings. I could go through all the topics, but I'm not. Truthfully, I remember why I stopped watching the show on a regular basis.

Watching the show, yesterday, helped me to see that there are things that we as parents tend to project on to our children. Whether good or bad, these projections affect our children and the adults that they become.

It is my aspiration to raise my children to be responsible, respectable, and reasonable god fearing adults. I want to be proud of them, but I also want them to be proud of themselves.

So…back to my question…Am I enough?

Like the cup of juice, there is a certain amount of juice in it, but it's up to the observer and their perspective to determine whether the glass is half empty or half full. I am choosing to look at my life and skills that I have been equipped with as…equipped. With that piece of knowledge I don't stop equipping myself with the tools that I need to continue to improve as a mother and wife, but I am equipped for the time.

I have to remind myself that God would not put more on me that I can bear and these four children are gifts from Him. He must have seen in me what I could not fully see yet, but still chose to make me a mother of four.

I'm not sure what makes good moms go bad or do bad things to their children, but I know that I trust the moral compass and Holy Spirit within me. I will continue to read, study, research, and enquire about the different parenting techniques of raising healthy children. I won't simply seek the teachings of the world, but that of the Bible because I know that the world is constantly changing its mind, but the Bible remains the same and so does God. As I grow and learn as an individual, it is my prayer that I will continue to be enough for my children.

If you are feeling the same way, I would encourage you to do an evaluation of yourself and then measure yourself through the word of God. If there are any ways in which you believe that you need to improve, ask God for the help. Seek the tools and answers to become better and move forward.

The more we work on being healthy people, spiritually, mentally, emotionally, and physically, the better parents we become for our children. In essence our becoming, becomes enough for them.

For it is precept upon precept,
Precept upon precept,
Line upon line,
Line upon line,
Here a little, there a little.
Isaiah 28:10

One Step at a Time

Last night was hard. With my husband being out if town for military duty, I found myself home alone with my kids. Now that's nothing new, but I by the end of the night, with all of its ups and downs, I was really stressed. I was going to do some school work, but I ended up passing out.

Now this morning wasn't much easier. My oldest son and I had to have a talk and that was stressful in itself. Now I'm sitting here thinking about the things that I need to get done for today and it seems like a lot.

Being a mother isn't always easy. There are times when it all feels like too much and those are the times that I have to take a step back and pray. If I'm completely honest, mothering isn't the only thing that feels like that, at times, but that's life.

I look forward to having a better day today, which means that I have to make it happen.

I'm getting ready to sit down at my trusty planner and write out my thoughts and plans for the day. Once I do that and confidently place one foot in front of the other, I know that God will take care of the rest.

In his heart a man plans his course, but the LORD determines his steps. Proverbs 16:9

This is my scripture for today. I have to remember that God is the one that will order things as I make plans.

Confidently, I give God all that I have today, knowing that He will take care of me and all that I have.

As stressful as yesterday was, today, I begin anew and refreshed. I take it upon myself to take authority in my life and not to allow any confusion. When it come in, I will not entertain it, but instead I will take a stand an move forward as God has called me to do in his word.

Behold, You delight in truth in the inward being, You teach me wisdom in the secret heart.
Psalm 51:6

It's not an easy job, but its mine

As a mother, I get to have fun with my children. I get to love on them and see them grow. I get hug and kiss them and say goodnight. I also get to make the hard decisions that they don't like.

As I sat with my children last night, I thought of all of the different things that present themselves to my children on a daily basis. My boys go to school and so this means that they see and hear a lot. Think of the children that come to school and talk about the things that they see at home. Then there are the teachers with their thoughts and opinions. While teaching my boys, I'm sure that their opinions are injected at times. My daughter faces these challenges and so much more.

Then there are the things that present themselves through various types of media…TV, radio, movies, books, video games, internet, etc...

As parents we are the filters that stand between our children and the content. We get to inspect and decide if the content is of a quality that we wish for our children to be exposed to.

I don't want my children to be like ostriches that have to stick their heads in the sand, but I want to present them with wholesome options for entertainment. We are training them and preparing them for their lives outside of our homes. What we allow to infiltrate the small minds today, will take up residence in their adult minds later on in life.

So, it a must that the content that my children take in, line up with the things that we believe and teach in our homes. As they grow older, we expose them to certain things and explain the various concepts to them. We have to help their minds develop in a healthy way. We don't allow the world to train our children because the world won't always tell the truth, especially when there is money involved.

Our children may not understand now, but one day they will. It isn't an easy job to do, but I am honored that it's mine and I'm proud to be their filter. I am also honored to have my husband beside me in this. There are times when he sees what I missed and as a team, we help our kids.

Today it is my prayer that God would help my husband and I to train up our children in the way that they should go, so that when they are old they will not depart from it. In Jesus' name. ~Amen

What do you think of this topic? Do you find yourself being a filter for your children or do you allow them to be their own filter?

The LORD looks down from heaven on the children of man, to see if there are any who understand, who seek after God
Psalm 14:2

All the fuss: 4th baby and birth control

I've been trying to decide if I wanted to write about this and I have decided that I do.

We recently had our fourth child. This is such a blessing, but we have been surrounded with comments from family members about this being our last. For some families, birth control and sterilization are very easy decisions, but it isn't that easy for us. It is just a nagging suggestion that everyone keeps in making. At least that's the way that I see it.

When I was in the hospital, the nurses kept in asking me what I planned on doing for birth control. They suggested everything from condoms to a hysterectomy. I thought this was very inconsiderate. I knew that they were concerned with the fact that this was my fourth child and that I had already had one C-section, but I wasn't pleased to have birth control pressured on me. I am not exaggerating. There were multiple nurses, about 5 or 6, that came into the room to discuss birth control with me. The thing that I find ironic is that they didn't make sure that I didn't have any questions about breastfeeding, the baby's umbilical cord, or anything else. It was assumed that I am an expert because this is my fourth. I guess I'm just a bit taken back by their assumptions regarding birth control.

What if we wanted a big family? What if we had our fourth child on purpose? What if we actually planned on having a quiver full? What if we were completely against the way that everyone else in the world thinks regarding birth control and family planning? They didn't consider any of this though. They just decided to pressure a new mother into some form of birth control. I must say, I am against this method of persuasion. I'm glad I'm strong in my beliefs.

It would be one thing if I didn't want any more children, but I just don't think that I should limit the size of my family based on some fear of not being a good mom, having enough money to raise them properly, other people's opinions, being those people with those kids, or having so many children that I never get to live my life. Instead I think the exact opposite.

I feel like God has blessed us with each one of our children. He also had provided us with all that we have needed to provide for them. Every time we have another child, we are blessed in our lives in a financial way that makes it possible to support them. I believe it happens this way because we depend on God to open doors and make the way for us to take care of our children. My husband does his job as a provider, I do my job as a nurturer, and God does his job as God. We trust him to do that. Yet, I don't expect other people who don't think the same way to see things from my perspective. Instead what I expect is a rendition of what they have done and all of their suggestions.

Almost every one we meet, every medical professional and family member suggests that we are done.

In all actuality, that decision is up to God. We are blessed because we have children. There are so many people out there in the world who pay thousands of dollars to have invetro-fertilization. The men want to know their sperm count and the women want to know if they are able to carry children. People adopt children because they haven't been able to conceive thus far. With all of this in mind, I refuse to convince myself that I should stop having children. We take care of our children and raise them well. I feel that God knows what's best. Besides, I love being a mother.

"Honor your father and mother, and, You shall love your neighbor as yourself"

Matthew 19:19

The Similarities

As I have mothered my children, I have often found similarities between their lives and my own.

I remember being at certain stages in my childhood and having such a great sense of innocence that the world was always beautiful and pure. I wondered why people would say that the world was evil. I asked my mother imposed certain restrictions upon me.

Then I became a mother. I realized that the world is not for us, it's against us, but God is. This realization showed me that God is more than able to protect us and our children. I have been shielded from so much.

As a child, we moved around a lot, but I realized one day that I was like a flower. As I was being watered and fed, my mother, by the wisdom of God, moved me to a place where the sunshine would hit me and help me grow.

She made sure that the environment that had bread great struggles for her were not mine to bear. Though times were not always easy, she helped me to be a woman that has faith. She showed me that I am beautiful and that I can do anything that I put my mind to and trust God for.

I look at my childhood and with all of its shinny bumps and bruises, I honour my mother for the patience she had in raising me.

My father, although not present in my home always took time to talk to me about the topics that mattered most. He kept my mind intrigued with complex, yet simple topics that would create an avid reader and learner.

Together they gave me the best parts of themselves and I'm thankful.

As I raise my children today, I think of my mother's wins and her loses. I learn from my father's blunders and his corrections. I see their goods and their bads and have chosen to use them as a way to be a good mother to my children.

You can't stay where you are. You have to move from that place.

You can't be afraid of what might come upon your children, if…

You just can't live that way.

Now, I am not speaking against wisdom, but I am speaking against tormenting fears that hold some moms captive. If you are that mother, you have to move past that place. If you are not that mother, you have to guard yourself against becoming her.

God said that He would protect our children. In Isaiah 54 He said, *"great shall be the peace of your children."* As I struggled with the past evils that many people have endured, I stood upon this scripture.

I had to see that God is more than able and willing to keep my kids safe. He is their Shelter. He is their Shield.

He is their Strong Tower and their Defence. He is the air that they breathe and the One that keeps them healthy.

Concerns of a mother never go away, but we cannot submit to the ways of the world or the enemy that tells us that our children have no hope. No!!!

This is a lie from the pit of hell. We have to look at what our children are watching and listening to and remove it, if it's unhealthy.

We have to teach them how to make the right choices, so that when they come across it again, they say "no" for themselves.

Train up a child in the way that he should go and when he is older, he won't depart from it.

This is true.

Face it. You won't have all of the answers, but you're not supposed to. God is.

That's where your love and direction comes from. He's who you point to.

Teach your children to pray and to study the word of God. Help them build relationships with God and later on, they will thank you.

I've thought about it and pondered over it. The thing that I have most like my mother is her faith that everything will be alright, because God is in control. I hope that my children are able to say the same.

10 Prayers to Pray for Your Children

    As a mother, with four children, I know that it is hard to send my babies out into the world. Daycare, school, events, none of this is easy. We are charged, as moms, with one of the best and hardest callings in the world. We are called to nurture and love our children; to help them become who God has created them to be. We carry our children within our wombs, as they grow. Once they are born, we raise them, as best as we know how, loving them and protecting them from danger. We teach them how to live. We show them how to love. We train them and coach them to be who God has created them to be.
Yet, we can't keep them in our physical arms forever.

    One of the first challenges of a working mother, a mother going to college, or even one that volunteers, is putting her baby in daycare. If a mother happens to avoid that one, she will soon face the challenge of sending her 4 or 5 year old to preschool or kindergarten. If a mother chooses to homeschool, she still does not escape the challenge of raising her child and slowly allowing him or her to go off into the world and explore through social connections. We haven't even talked about high school, college, or adulthood.

    We hear the news reports. They aren't fun to listen to or read. Children go through so much today and it is very public. Turn on the nightly news and hear of manipulation, abuse, scandal, kidnappings. If one is not careful, a mother could have a panic attack trying to figure out how she could protect her babies from all of these troubles and more befalling them.

Will they become sick? She wonders, am I a good mother? Will I do them any justice? However, she forgets one thing. It is not her call to protect her child all of the time, throughout the entire duration life. She is not God.

However, she forgets one thing. She is not God.

She has to do what the Bible says.

Be anxious for nothing, but in everything by prayer and supplication, with thanksgiving, let your requests be made known to God; 7 and the peace of God, which surpasses all understanding, will guard your hearts and minds through Christ Jesus. ~Philippians 4:6, 7

We can all use a little peace. Add with the stress of the world and the cares of this life, we could definitely use a lot of peace. This peace does not just come. You have to do something in order for this peace to even begin to come your way. You have to be willing to give God the things that you are most concerned about. In this case, your children and their futures need to handed over to the Lord. I want to help with this today.

There are key scriptures that I have prayed over my children for the past 14 years. When situations arise and fear attempts to grip me, I have to remind myself of what the Lord has said. He would not leave me nor forsake me. (Deuteronomy 31:6) I have had to speak, pray, and meditate on the promises of God. I have to remind myself that God is faithful and that all the promises of God in Him *are* Yes, and in Him Amen, to the glory of God through us. (2 Corinthians 1:20) I have to praise Him, when I recognize His faithfulness. So, what exactly does His word promise? I am going to share 10 prayers with you that are directly related to the scriptures in the bible and God's promises to us, who believe. The prayers are in bold and the scriptural references follow them. When you pray these prayers, pray them out loud. Get them ingrained in your heart, so that you pray them with faith and without any doubt. (James 1:8)

- **Lord let my children be taught by You and give them great peace. Let all who have a hand in teaching them, be ordained by you.** Isaiah 54:13 "All of your children shall be taught by the Lord, and great shall be the peace of your children."

- **Lord keep my children safe from all hurt, harm, and danger. Place your hedge of protection around them. Let no evil befall them and no plague or calamity come near to their dwelling. Keep them safely under the shadow of Your mighty wing of protection.** Psalm 91:10 "No evil shall befall you, nor shall any plague come near your dwelling" (I recommend that you read all of Psalm 91)

- **Lord bless my children, for they are the fruit of my body. Give them increase as you have given increase to me.** Deuteronomy 28:4 "Blessed shall be the fruit of your body, the produce of your ground and the increase of your herds, the increase of your cattle and the offspring of your flocks."

- **Lord help my children to be strong and courageous. Let no man be able to stand before them, all of the days of their lives. Be with them as you were with Moses and remind them that you will never leave them or forsake them. Bless them with the fruit of the spirit. Let them not be overtaken by fear, but instead allow them to live in power, in love, and with a sound mind.** Joshua 1:5 "No man shall be able to stand before you all the days of your life; as I was with Moses, so I will be with you. I will not leave you nor forsake you. " Galatians 5:22-23; 2 Timothy 1:7; 1 Corinthians 15:33

- **Let each one of my children, (Insert names here), increase in wisdom and in stature and in favor with You, God, and with man, even as Jesus did. Let them keep good company because you said in Your word that bad company corrupts good character.** Luke 2:52 "And Jesus increased in wisdom and in stature and in favor with God and man."
- **Father, all of the days of their lives, give them a heart to delight themselves in You, Lord; and give them the desires of their hearts.** Psalm 37:4 "Delight yourself also in the Lord, and He will give you the desires of your heart."
- **As they grow and learn, give them wisdom Lord. No matter if they turn to the right or to the left, let their ears hear Your voice behind them saying, "This is the way; walk in it," and may they follow you all of the days of their lives because you are their Shepherd.** Isaiah 30:21 Whether you turn to the right or to the left, your ears will hear a voice behind you, saying, "This is the way; walk in it." Psalm 23
- **Father I ask you to forgive all of their iniquities, heal all of their diseases, redeem their lives from destruction, clothe them with lovingkindness and tender mercies, satisfy their mouths with good things, and renew them continually.** Psalm 103
- **Help them to retain the knowledge of You, God, and do not give them over to a reprobate mind. Instead, keep their minds, by the power of your Holy Spirit. Let no weapon formed against them prosper and every tongue that rises up against them in judgement be condemned. Help them continually to put on the armor of God that they may be able to stand against the wiles of the devil.** Ephesians 6:10-

18; Romans 1:28; Ephesians 1:13; John 17:11-12; Isaiah 54:17

- **Help me and those that you have ordained, to train them up in the way that they should go, so that they will not depart from that way, when they are older. If you have it for my child/children to be married, prepare a spouse for my child and prepare my child. I pray that they would both love you, Lord and not be given over to sinful pleasures or the works of the flesh. I come against the spirit of fornication, sexual immorality, divorce, confusion, rejection, and separation on behalf of my child and his/her future marriage, right now. In the name of Jesus, I tell these mountains to move and I believe that they shall be moved. In Jesus name, I pray all of these things. Amen** Proverbs 22:6; 2 Corinthians 6:14; Acts 10:2; Ephesians 5:18; Matthew 22:37; Matthew 21:21; 1 Corinthians 6:18-20; Hebrews 13:4; 1 Corinthians 7:2

Rest assured that God will hear each one of your prayers.

Pray them in faith, knowing that He cares about you and everyone & thing the you care about. I tell you this; the Lord is faithful. He is not a man that He should lie and like one of my favorite scriptures says, if you put your faith and trust in the Lord, you will not be put to shame. (Romans 10:11)

I would recommend that you pray these prayers over your children daily. Watch as the Lord fulfills His promises to you and your children.

*The lions may grow weak and hungry,
but those who seek the L*ORD *lack no good thing.*
Psalm 34:10

Dear New Mom,

Today, I thought of you.

I thought of your ambition. I thought of your desire to be the best mother that you could possibly be. I thought of the dreams that you have for your child. As I thought of you, I thought of the journey that you are going to take as your child grows older.

Each day will give you something new. There will be opportunities to be your best and your worst, but I encourage you to be your best. Even when you find that you have not done that, don't beat yourself up. Stop…take a minute and ask God to forgive and help you. Ask Him for wisdom, and then forgive yourself. Allow yourself to make mistakes. We all do it. This life is full of chances to grow and being a mother is one of them.

Your child's will help you develop patience. Your patience will help your child develop character.
If you find that you need help, don't be afraid to ask. Everyone has moments when they cannot do it all on their own. You are not weak, dumb, or less than because you need some assistance.

Remember that your child is a gift. No matter how you feel, remind yourself that God gave that precious baby to you. Although there are times when you may feel clueless, remember that all mothers have felt that way. You are not the only one. Everything that you need to raise your child has been place in you by God. He will help you to do it if you ask.

Today, my thoughts and prayers go out to you. Remember to take a breath. You have to breathe.

Rest…You have to rest. Be…don't try, just be. Today, I pray that you would be strengthened…that you would laugh…and if you cry, that you would feel free, knowing that God caught each prayer encompassed in the tears.

Today, I want to encourage you. You are enough. Hold on! Don't let go! Don't be afraid, you are not alone. Find a way to have fun and when that voice in your head tells you that you can't do it, tell it to shut up. Give this your all and you will see your fruit turn into someone that brings you great joy.
Sincerely,
Makeda

Some of Life's Lessons

Wisdom calls aloud outside;
She raises her voice in the open squares.
Proverbs 1:20

No Longer Moved

We all have a propensity for self-doubt.

It is a part of our human nature. We live and we learn. Sometime we win and sometimes we lose. However, these situations are not and cannot become an indicator to ourselves nor to anyone else of who we are.

I used to be afraid of the judgements of men. By men, I mean people. I use to wonder what everyone would think of what I said, did, and thought.

I lived in the constant bondage and fear of being rejected. No matter how sure I was of what I was doing, somehow, I still doubted that it would be approved.

What I learned over the years was that I was looking for approval from the wrong source.

I wanted people, in their own frailty of human nature, to approve what I was doing and who I was.

I was ignorant of the fact that real approval cannot come from mortals. It can only come from the One who has the power to judge all.

I studied hard to show myself approved to men. All the while wondering why God had not showed who I was to them. I must admit, looking back, I missed it. I was never meant to study to show myself approved to men. I was to study and work and live and move and be to show myself approved to God. For He is the

One that stamps me with the seal of approval. And while I was seeking the approval of men, God was cheering me on in my everyday endeavors as a woman, a wife, and a mother.

Yet again, I would miss it. I had not allowed His words to penetrate my being. I looked at who had walked away and forgotten about me. I looked to who had said I was not enough and I wasn't qualified.

I missed it.

I should have been looking to the One who called me and qualified me. I should have looked to the One who was there and always remains; the One who said, I was and still am enough.

Today, I am able to share this because I have been through some trials and hardships. I have been hurt and realized that I allowed men and women to change what God had made in me. I have learned from my struggles and from the LOVE OF GOD.

I am no longer moved by the looks, judgements, and harsh words of people. I am different because I am loved.

Today, I want to challenge you to see if you can relate. Look into your past and see if there were times and situations that caused you to forget who you were and feel less confident. See if you have ever replaced God's approval with the desire of being approved by men. As you do this, realize that you need not to look to this earth any more for approval.

You are loved.

He shall be like a tree
Planted by the rivers of water,
That brings forth its fruit in its season,
Whose leaf also shall not wither;
And whatever he does shall prosper.
Psalms 1:3

Allowing the Word of God to Change Your Mind and Renew it

If you are like me, living in the 21st century, which I assume by the fact that you are reading this, that you are, there are situations that come up all of the time that warrant your opinion. This may not be a public warrant, but there is an inward conversation that takes place.

Just stop to think for a moment.

When changes are happening in your life, community, and the world, you have an opinion. You may not clearly understand or express this opinion to anyone, but have it. I want to ask you a question. What is your opinion based on? Is it based on facts, the past, your hurts, or the Word of God?

Some people would be inclined to say that their opinions are based on truth, but truth, unless godly is subjective. There is THE truth, but most situations are based on an occurrence that can be understood differently depending on the perspective of the viewer. This is now what I am asking you to consider.

I want you to think about the foundations of your opinions because I want to convince you that it is more prosperous to base your opinions on things that cannot be changed or shaken, like the Word of God…THE TRUTH.

I am currently working on a post to be published to my website because one of my readers asked me a question. This question was an opinion based question, but the truth about me is that I try not to express my opinions unless I know the stand that the Bible takes on it. Thus, I am taking a bit longer to write it, than I expected.

I have to research the topic and pray for guidance. I learned this a long time ago. When I had just gotten married and became a mother, I was full of my own opinions. God was in the process of changing me and having my own opinions, based on my truth, made it hard for the change to transpire within me. I found that I had to submit my will and opinions to the Lord, through the Word of God, in order for the change to happen. That's why I began to acknowledge my own opinions, but give myself permission to change them based on the word of God.

I found that I needed to have the authority of the unchanging Word to solidify my thoughts and beliefs. No one can change God or the TRUTH of His Word. When we stand on His solid foundation, we are strengthened and become confident in who He is and what He has said. This in turn makes us better and renews our minds.

And do not be conformed to this world, but be transformed by the renewing of your mind, that you may prove what is that good and acceptable and perfect will of God. ~Romans 12:2

This renewal process that takes place within our minds changes our entire being. Our lives become proving ground for the perfect will of God. We become His living examples of what He finds to be acceptable and good. This is hard to do when we are stuck in our own ways.

Don't want to let go of your opinion? That is what is going to continue to lead you all the days of your life.

If you are being led by your own opinion, someone may come to you with their own truth. That person may be more confident, older, or more experienced. They may have a strong presence that commands your attention and demands you to reconsider their perspectives. If this happens, you are or can become completely shaken. Do you know what happens when you and your thoughts are shaken? You become a double minded man.

For let not that man suppose that he will receive anything from the Lord; he is a double-minded man, unstable in all his ways. ~James 1:7, 8

Do you remember that I was telling you about being more prosperous because of the fact that you have chosen to submit your opinions to the Lord? Well this is where the prosperity comes in handy. You can't receive anything from God when you are double minded.

You are praying and praying; crying out to the Lord. Yet, you see no fruit from your labor.

Do you wonder why? Well the Bible says that you ask amiss. And a lot of times it's because you asked, but you didn't do what the Lord told you to do. There is a prerequisite. He tells you. Do not be conformed to the world. Renew your mind. Do not expect anything from the Lord, when you have chosen to be double-minded and unstable in your ways.

You have to choose the Lord's way.

Do you want Him to open doors for you or do you want to go beating down the doors yourself?

I would choose to allow the Lord to do it. I've tried it the other way and it doesn't work. When you beat on doors, you hurt your hands and your feelings get hurt.

This Book of the Law shall not depart from your mouth, but you shall meditate in it day and night, that you may observe to do according to all that is written in it. For then you will make your way prosperous, and then you will have good success. ~Joshua 1:8

Do you see that? You have to meditate on the word of God. You have to keep it in your mouth, both day and night. You have to watch and observe to do all that it says. This is how you will prosper. Not by following every wind of doctrine of every so called celebrity or successful guru that comes your way. Not even from being strong and wise in your own eyes.

Start listening to people that base their foundational thoughts and lives upon the word of God; people who don't mind saying that they were wrong; people who do as they believe.

As you fill your mind, time, and relationships according to the Word of God, doors will open. You will see that your life will take a new turn. You will be more satisfied and, I know, that you will be changed for the better.

If you are wondering how to get started with this process, I suggest that you simply spend time reading the word of God. From there you can begin to hear and recognize the voice of God. Then you will be ready to study the word. Just remember that becoming the woman that God desires you to be is not a quick journey. It is a lifetime full of experiences that change as you change and are obedient to the Lord.

*Blessed is the man
Who walks not in the counsel of the ungodly,
Nor stands in the path of sinners,
Nor sits in the seat of the scornful;
But his delight is in the law of the L*ORD,
*And in His law he meditates day and night.
Psalms 1:1, 2*

A Week of Lessons

It is the end of the week and the first week of a new season, in my life. I have spent the entire week doing all that was required of me and more. My children just went back to school on Monday and I started a new semester in graduate school. Not only that, but I am now in a new program/college, so I'm having to adjust to how things work. With all that has been going on, I have not been able to write as I had desired, but I did take some time to reflect on a few lessons from this week. Some were new lessons and others were reiterated lessons. I just want to share a few of these with you.

These lessons have come from specific areas of my life, but I think that there are ways that they can be applied in multiple areas as well.

As a Woman

With all of the busy-ness in the air, I had to make sure that I stayed on track with what was happening around me. There are six people in my family and it is very easy for me to be the last one that is taken care of. However, when that happens, no one is happy because I am tired and drained. I can't really support them the way that I need and want to. This is why I've had to pray for wisdom and to use it.

Here are a few of the lessons that I've learned as a woman. Perhaps, you will find them helpful.

Always have a plan

I don't know about you, but when too much is happening in my brain, things don't go well. I am not able to give the current situation 100% because I am too busy being concerned about the other 5 things that I have to do. I may run late or even forget about some other the things that need to be done. For this reason, I believe that it is important to take time, every day or the night before, to make a plan.

I believe that it is important to take time, every day or the night before, to make a plan.

Not only do I make a plan, but I get that plan out of my head and onto paper. This gives me a reference point and allows me to focus on the task at hand. This week having a plan, definitely came in handy. My oldest is in high school, my two middle children are in elementary, and I still have a toddler at home. I still want to maintain my relationship with my husband and other close family and friends. Being scatter brain would definitely not help my relationships.

Plan, but Be Flexible

Although I have a plan, I can't be rigid and stuck in that plan. There are a few different reasons for this. The first one is the most important. I have shared this before, but I personally know it to be true.

The mind of man plans his way, but the Lord directs his steps. ~Proverbs 16:9

No matter what plan we have, we are not sovereign or God. He has an ultimate plan for our lives and while He does desire for us to plan our way, it is ultimately His direction that we will walk in. I can set 9,900 tasks to complete for the day, but the Lord knows those which I will really accomplish. This is why we must remain flexible. We have to know that He has it all together, even when we do not.

Planning allows us to steward our day. However, flexibility leaves room for the things that God has orchestrated to happen. Let's be honest… the reality of it is that whether we decide to remain flexible or not, the Lord will have His way and things will happen.

It is just better to plan to be flexible, so that we are able to cope with the change well. When people don't cope with change well, they begin to experience anxiety because things did not go the way that they intended for them to go.

But the question is, who is in charge here, us or God?

We must steward, but remain humble and flexible enough to receive His plan for our lives.

This leads to the other reason for flexibility. Things come up. People need us. Schedules change and sometimes, we just need to rest. Allowing ourselves to remain flexible does not cancel out the plan; it is just the realistic part of planning.

If we remain flexible, things will go better and life will remain enjoyable…trust me on this one. I know from experience.

Eat Healthy & Stay Rejuvenated

Whenever I talk to my father about things that are happening in my life, before we begin to assess the situation, he always asks me a few questions about my state of mind and my health.

1 Did you eat and take your vitamins
2 Were you well rested or tired
3 Did you exercise or stretch/meditate (in the word of God), or do your affirmations

The point of his questions is not that of the specific details of the activities. Instead, he is simply asking me if I had taken care of myself this morning or prior to the event that we are about to discuss. After years of my father asking me these questions, I began to realize the difference in my mood when I had taken the opportunity to take care of myself and when I had not.

I began to realize the difference in my mood when I had taken the opportunity to take care of...

In those times when I had neglected self-care, I would find that I was more irritable and frustrated. However, when I had taken the time to do what I needed to do to take care of myself, I functioned better. My family and friends were more pleased with my presence and everyone is happier.

This week, this was very important. With having to run so many errands and adjusting to the new schedule that we have, making sure that I took my vitamins, rested at night, exercised and took time to meditate on the Word of God, were keys to my week going well. I honestly believe that this is one of the reasons why I am not completely drained or frustrated at the end of the week.

Tests Will Come, but Prayer is Essential

All week, we dealt with different situations. There were new adjustments that my children had to make with their sleeping, eating, and playing schedules because of school. They had new teachers and friends. My schedule took a beating, as we all had to get up earlier and be on a well-structured schedule.

On top of the normal things, policies at the schools raised questions that needed our attention. My textbooks did not arrive on time, which put me behind in my coursework. When I contacted UPS, the manager told me that my books were "in a box, on a plane somewhere, about to land and be delivered to me in 24 hours."

Situations like this come up and we have to decide how to handle them. I had to pray a lot this week. My children were dealing with situations with their friends and teachers, while I was dealing with my University. I could have easily lost my temper, but I decided to seek God prior to moving forward with all of my actions.

This did not require an hour-long prayer. I just simply stopped what I was doing and asked God to help me. I asked Him to lead me, guide me, and direct me, as to what I should do next. Then, I moved forward.

Later on, I took more time to submit the details of my concerns to God in prayer.

The great thing about God is that He is very faithful. When I asked Him for help, He helped me. There were a few situations that He had me to request further attention from the supervisors and others that He directed me to, simply, leave alone.

I wanted to make sure that I was using my time and energy the right way, so I just did what He led me to do. I must say, life was less emotional than I know it could have been, if I had done it all my way.

Rest, Reflection, & Relationships are Key

As a woman, I am a relational being. In many ways I could be considered an extrovert, but I have my introvert ways about me as well. I like to say that I am me, but I realize that "me" doesn't help you understand what I'm trying to say.

Rest

I spent a lot of time doing and going this week, but as much as it was important that I plan and execute the plan, it was equally important that I rest and reflect on the situations of life.

Each morning, I take the time to sit down and do nothing. I might sit outside in my chair and read or I may stay inside. Yet, I give myself the opportunity to do nothing. If I choose not to read, I just observe the atmosphere and take in the moment of the day.

I have found that this is an essential part to my functionality throughout the day. I realized it even more so this week. No matter what was going on, I had already given myself the time that I needed to rest.

Reflection

Generally, I take some time to sit down and write out my thoughts regarding the previous day's activities. Very early on in my marriage, motherhood, and life as a woman, I found that it was beneficial to write out my thoughts. This gave me the opportunity to think about the things that were happening in my life without having to share every detail of my being with another individual. While I have trusted relationships, reflection brings about self-awareness and studies have shown that those who are more self-aware are also very aware of others. As we come to know more about who we are, we learn more about the difference between us and God, ourselves and others, and life.

Reflection on life is essential to personal growth. It is one of the reasons why, I believe, that my season of life has changed as it has. If I had not realized specific things about life and my situations, I would not be able to adjust accordingly to the changes that God was wanting to bring about in me. My character has definitely benefited from reflection.

Relationships

It is not good for us to be alone. This is something that God made very clear, early on in the book of Genesis. We are supposed to have relationship with God, family, and friends. Yet, many times the busy-ness of life drowns out the time for relationships. However, I have found that it is very important to remember that not only do we need relationship with others, but they need relationship with us a well.

My husband and children not only desire my cooking and driving skills. They also desire to have my time and attention. This is one of the reasons why I have not been on social media as much as I have in the past. The clicking and ticking of my fingers hitting the keyboard should not outweigh the amount of time that I spend with my family.

I also have friends that are such a great blessing to my life. They are wise, funny, smart, and caring women of God. I am so honored that God has given them to me and I have come to realize that relationships have to be cultivated in order to grow. If they are not cultivated, they will remain as they are and in some situations, they may even die.

Thus, in the midst of all that I have going on in my life, as a woman, I will continue to make time for relationships.

Next Lessons

I did not know that this post would be so long and I don't want to overwhelm you with too many details, so I am going to make my Parenting Tips and Marriage Tips of the Week very brief. Perhaps, I can expand on these in the near future.

As A Wife

I have noticed that no matter how busy life can get there are specific things that I can do to maintain and improve my relationship with my husband. Here are a few of my tips for the week.

    1   **Listen & Encourage**– Many times, my husband just wants me to listen to him. Many times, my husband just wants me to listen to him   He isn't looking for me to tell him what to do or how to do it. He just wants to have me as an open ear and heart that is on his side. I take his concerns to the Lord and allow Him to be all that my husband needs. Then, when the opportunity is right and I see that there is room for it, I encourage my husband. Perhaps I just share with him the fact that I appreciate him as a husband, father, and friend. I could also communicate to him through my embrace that he is respected and loved. I find that these two things are very important to building a healthy and prosperous relationship with my husband.

    2   **Be Available**– With all that I have going on, it is important that I make time for my husband. This might mean that I remain flexible throughout my day to do or be there for him, when he requests it. Now his requests may not always be verbal, but I have to pay attention to the requests that he makes.

Allowing myself to remain available to my husband affords us the ability to continue to grow. With this he is continually reminded that I am trustworthy, dependable, and faithful to him. (Of course there are times when I cannot pull away from a meeting or something of that nature, but I must communicate that I will get back to him as soon as I am free.)

      3   **Find Something to Laugh About–** Life is tough enough. We don't want to go through the moments without a friend to laugh with. There is no better partner for this than your husband. Listen attentively to his jokes and laugh, when you find them funny. Try to be light-hearted and care free at times. Tickle, wrestle, or just poke him. If he isn't a touchy type of guy, find ways that you two can laugh together. Laughter makes the heart healthy and brightens up a relationship. Sometimes, my husband and I just look at each other and start to giggle because, well…it's silly. It helps our relationship to stay fun and can become useful in the moments when times are hard. This week, it was important for us to laugh together. We were so busy and had so many different situations come up that laughing gave us a breath of fresh air.

As A Parent

My tips of the week as a parent are very simple, self-explanatory, and effective.

      1   **Listen well–** Make sure to pay attention to your children when they are speaking to you. Make eye contact and actively listen to what they are saying. This builds their confidence and helps them to know that they are loved.

      2   **Make time for your children–** This means that sometime we have to say no to something else, but making time for our children allows us to do things with them that brings the quality above the quantity. Perhaps you could read a book, color a picture, toss the football, or play hopscotch. Doing these things with our children show them that we care and make it so that they don't feel deprived of our attention

3   Just Be There. It Means A LOT– Sometimes there isn't anything to do. Our children want to play with their friends, watch television, or read by themselves. However, the fact that we are in the room makes them feel loved and secure. I have seen this with my children. It is especially true when they spend 8 hours or more, away from my husband and I, in the presence of other adults that are not family. This also helps them to feel confident.

Have I not commanded you? Be strong and of good courage; do not be afraid, nor be dismayed, for the L<small>ORD</small> your God is with you wherever you go."
Joshua 1:9

How Do I Wait?

Have you ever been in the midst of a situation and wasn't sure of the direction that you should move in?

Perhaps you are currently in a season of your life where you are waiting on God to make your direction clear.

If this is you, I know from experience that this could be a bit frustrating. You are probably wondering "How am I supposed to wait?"

I'll tell you how. **Patiently.**

Ok…wait. Hear me out. I know that you may not want to wait and you might be very frustrated. However, I also know that while you are waiting on God, patience is building in you, He is clearing the path before you, and He will guide your steps as you move forward.

How do I know these things? Well, the Bible makes it very clear that the steps of a righteous man are ordered by the Lord.(Psalm 37:23) It also says that those that wait upon the Lord shall have renewed strength. They shall mount up on wings as eagles. They shall walk and not be weary. They shall run and not faint.(Isaiah 40:31) Plus, if you just think about it, waiting produces patience and the patience produces character.(Romans 5:4) The Lord goes before you,(Deuteronomy 31:8) when you trust Him. He sets your feet firmly upon a rock, so that you won't slip.(Psalm 40:2) He also guides your steps, when you acknowledge Him in all of your ways. (Proverbs 3:6)

Wait a moment. Let's stop right here. When you find a scripture that has a promise and a contingency, it is important to understand what the contingency requires of you. The reason for this is that if you do not do your part, the promise will not be fulfilled.

For this particular promise, the Word of God tells us that God will direct our steps, if we acknowledge Him in all our ways. It actually says it this way.

In all of your ways acknowledge Him and He will direct your path. ~Proverbs 3:6

You have to know that Lord keeps His word. He isn't a man that He should lie. (Numbers 23:19) You don't have to think that focusing upon the Lord and doing things according to His word are tedious actions that will get you nowhere. Instead, you must realize that everyone who stands upon the Word of God in life and focuses on the things of God, seeking first His kingdom and righteousness, will have all of the things that they need and want added to them. (Matthew 6:33, Psalm 34:10)

So where am I going with this? I'll tell you where I'm going.

Remember how you were waiting on God to do something? You were wondering about the path that your feet would take in life. Will you meet those goals? Will you accomplish those dreams? Will you reach your full potential? Will you make the wrong move or the right turn? Remember this, it is the Lord that is working in you, both to will and to do for His good pleasure.(Philippians 2:13) As long as you give yourself over to Him and focus on Him, acknowledging Him in **all** of your ways, He will direct your steps.

Ok now wait…

Someone one out there is wondering why this is a good thing. They have heard really horrific stories about God leading His people into tragedies and some really troubling situations. They have been afraid of the big man sitting in a chair in the heavens, ready to punish someone with his lightening rod.

Let me tell you this, that's not an image of God. That is an image is Zeus, a Greek polytheistic view of an idol/Titan; again not God.

God longs to be gracious to us. (Isaiah 30:18) He has a plan and a future for you (Jeremiah 29:10) He is good to those who hope in Him. (Lamentations 3:25) He delivers those that seek Him.

I challenge you today to stop and read Psalms 103. Look at the qualities of our God ask yourself if you had the correct image of Him in your mind. I am telling you to do this because sometimes we don't. This incorrect image can stop us from trusting Him, waiting upon Him, and knowing that He cares.(1 Peter 5:7)

Remember, there is something for us to do in order not to take the wrong path. We must trust in the Lord, patiently wait on Him, and acknowledge Him in all of our ways. As we do this, we will begin to seek Him and our paths will be made straight.

I don't know about you, but that should make you confident in how you live your life.

I hope you found encouragement in this today and will trust in the Lord as you **patiently** wait on Him.

If you have to choose one Bible verse to focus on after reading this post, let it be Proverbs 3:6 "In all of your ways **acknowledge Him** and He **will direct** your path."

But seek first the kingdom of God and His righteousness, and all these things shall be added to you.
Matthew 6:33

The Little Things...

Over the past 13 ½ years, I have gone from working mom, to student, and then to stay at home mom and back to student/SAHM again. When I look at the standard that the world sets, I realize am supposed to be able to do it all and still live a healthy life as a wife and mother. However, I have found this to be a task that I have not successfully achieved in all of my adult life, to the degree that I desire.

When I attempt to tackle too much, I find that I am overwhelmed by the daily tasks and expectations that are set before me. I want to be, both, a great wife and a great mother, but when working hard at achieving these two goals and then trying to juggle a full time job, it seems that I end up dropping the ball and despising one aspect of my life.

For that very reason, I decided to give up the 9-5 for a while. I decided to focus on my education, which will afford me the opportunity work on a more flexible schedule while doing what I love. In the mean time I focus on being thankful for the little things.

What little things? You ask…

1. I am thankful for the conflicts that my husband and I have. They remind me that I am in a healthy relationship where my spouse is willing to challenge me. He helps to sharpen me like iron and he makes me better. **I am married.**

2. I am thankful for the mandate that I have to balance my roles as mother and wife with other roles that I have. They remind me of how important it is to me to be a mother and a wife. These challenges show me that somethings will come up against my most important human relationships, but resilience and reevaluation are the keys to getting things back in line. **I am a wife and a mother.**

3. I am thankful for the mounds of laundry that I tend to have. We have six people in our family and those mounds of laundry remind me that God has blessed us with tons of clothes and choices of what to wear. **We have clothes to wear.**

4. I am thankful for the dishes in my sink. I have to take the time to wash them, either by hand or by dishwasher, but they remind me that we have all eaten and do so daily. **We have food to eat.**

5. I am thankful for the toys to pick up off of the floor. They remind me that God has blessed us with an income to provide for our children's pleasure. They get to play with things that they enjoy. **We have a steady income and material things to enjoy.**

6. I am thankful for the time that I have to manage wisely. As a stay at home mom, I have a certain amount of time that I have to manage in order to be productive, while my family is away at school and work. This could feel overwhelming at times, but it is a blessing to have that time to decide what I would like to take care of and how I would like to do it. **I am still alive and can manage my time.**

7. I am thankful that I have to tell my kids to stop running around the house or being so loud. I grew up as an only child in my house, so I having four children actively running around and playing are things that I had to get used to. However, their noise is a very pleasant reminder that they are healthy and

adventurous. Their noise and lively activities remind me that I have been blessed with children and I am thankful. **I have children and they are healthy.**

8. I am also thankful for the school work that I have to complete and the books that I have to read. They are reminders of the fact that I am receiving an education that will prepare me of various opportunities in life. **I have the opportunity to be educated and make the best out of life. I have a sound mind.**

I have a long list of things that I could discuss, but I think you get the jest of what I'm saying. It is very hard to forget our blessings, especially when some of our struggles come from those very places. We could all take a look at the things that we complain about and realize that they are simply a blessing that we must learn how to manage.

Do you have various areas of your life, where you tend to complain, but after reading this, realize that you have more to be thankful for than to complain about?

Trust the Lord

Your Relationships

*Now to Him who is able to do exceedingly
abundantly above all that we ask or think,
according to the power that works in us,
Ephesians 3:20*

Keep on Going

There are times when I am tired. I am tired of all of the mundane things that occur in the midst of a relationship.

Some people don't realize what it takes to maintain a relationship with someone that you love. It doesn't just come together and work out smoothly without some sort of effort and work. Still, we are human and we will get tired.

I know that you understand what I mean. I believe that you find yourself drained, at times, and want to throw in the towel.

It happens with everything in life. It happens in friendships, marriages, parenting, work, and even in things that we enjoy the most, our hobbies. We are often faced with the challenge of quitting and our next step will determine the outcome of the situation.

That's where I am. I'm trying to make sure that I don't make a stupid decision. I don't want to my emotions to cause me to make a life altering decision that I can't take back. Still, I will admit, we need some help.

All people do, especially in relationships, but we need some intervention from God.

I know that I need him to help me have faith in Him to work out my concerns with my relationship. I'm sure that He will. It's just not easy remaining positive when things aren't always "good."

Until things become better, I'll just have to keep pressing on. I'll have to keep on going.

And do not be conformed to this world, but be transformed by the renewing of your mind, that you may prove what is that good and acceptable and perfect will of God.

Romans 12:2

Why Encourage Other People

As people we are all boggled down with life. We get so busy doing the things that we think are necessary and required. When we are not doing the necessary and required, we begin to do what we desire. Sometimes we fail to realize or just forget that we live in a community of people that need us…and we need them.

Whether we are thinking about our home, family, friends, neighbors, church, online community, or even, dare I say, the world…we all need each other. When individuals spend too much time alone, they begin to experience thoughts that may not be conducive to their "best" life. In the Bible, this loneliness or not having encouragement, led to disbelief because people started to question the faith that they once had in God. (Hebrews 3) This is the reason why God tells us to exhort one another.

We have to be there, available, ready, and willing to encourage our brothers and sisters in the faith. We have no idea the struggles that they are going through and no one has any idea what we are going through as well. But God…

He is more that aware of our present condition and yes, He does and will encourage us, but He also gave us one another. We are a family and He wants us to help each other in our weakness.

If you are losing hope…don't. Period…

God says in His word that no one who trust in and puts their hope in Him will ever be put to shame. (Romans 10:11)

If you feel like things are impossible…stop. Period…

God says in His word that with Him all things are possible. (Matthew 19:26)

If you feel like you have to give in to sin and temptation…don't feel that way. And run!!! Period.

God says in His word that although sin comes to our house and knocks on the door, it crouches and waits; we have power over that sin…to overcome it. (Genesis 4:7, James 4:7)

If you feel that the cares in your life are just too much to bear and God doesn't even care…like a car coming to a screeching holt, I say…DO NOT FEEL THAT WAY. Period…

God tells us in His word that he cares for us. In fact, He wants us to thrust our cares upon Him because He cares. That's right! He cares about everything that we care about. (1 Peter 5:7)

I am suggesting that you can just stop all of the things that I mentioned above. We have to take control of our emotions and cast vain thoughts out of our minds and vain imaginations off of us. (2 Corinthians 10:5)

We have to tell ourselves (sometimes speaking out loud) that the thoughts and feelings that attempt to settle in us that are contrary to what God says and who He is, are all vain. Therefore, there is no need to hold on to them. We have to verbally cast them off!

Do you see how this works? I am encouraging you. Somehow, in encouraging you, I too, feel myself being encouraged. Why? Because we are the body of Christ and we need to build one another up so that or body can be strong. We are more connected that you know.

If one of us veers off to the left or the right, there are ravenous wolves waiting to devour…these are seen and unseen. Our thoughts and feelings are used as catalysts and springboards to set our hearts in motion away from or towards God.

So today let's stir one another up. Let's encourage one another in the faith. Let's encourage one another in relationships, work, hobbies, and life. God has empowered us to do it. Someone might give up and turn away because we didn't encourage him or her. That's what the Bible says.

Be uniquely you, have no fear, and encourage someone else. You never know what a smile and a good word will do.

Confess your trespasses to one another, and pray for one another, that you may be healed. The effective, fervent prayer of a righteous man avails much.
James 5:16

I Prayed for You

I said a prayer late at night
I prayed for you when things didn't seem right
Prayed when you were lost
I prayed for you and then I trusted God
I prayed for you when I heard you cry for help
I prayed for you when you no longer looked like yourself
I prayed and kept praying, hoping for a change
I prayed and cried out His name
I prayed for you asking God to save you
From the thing that would kill you
Destroy you and shame you
I prayed and asked God not to blame you
You had no idea what you were in
You could not recognize the magnitude of your sin
I hoped that I could be proud of you one day
I prayed because sadness filled my heart when the world
called you out of your name
I prayed for you like you were my sister
Long lost and afraid, far away in the distance
And although I've said that I've prayed, I'm still praying
Hoping for the change
One day you'll see it all, when you come to that age
Age of willingness to seek the Lord
His will and desire for your life
Don't pull away from him contingent in strife
I am hoping and praying for you although we are not friends
Hoping and praying that you'll be alright in the end.

For the Scripture says, "Whoever believes on Him will not be put to shame."
Romans 10:11

Final Thoughts from the Author

As I was writing this book, praying, and seeking God about the direction that it should take He impressed something upon me that I want you to know. As a woman, wife, and mother, I have had to work harder on these areas than I ever had on anything else in my life. There have literally been moments when I wanted to quit, but I couldn't because of love. I love God. I love my husband. I love my children. I love all of those that I have not met that will come from my bloodline.

This experience of being this woman has caused me to become resilient. The enemy has thrown a lot my way, but God has always kept me. Life does not get easier. If you are going to fight, you better make sure that it is worth fighting for. Your marriage and your children are worth fighting for. Your integrity as a godly woman is worth fighting for.

Knowing this, please always remember that you have to keep on praying. You have to always be seeking and submitting yourself to God. You always have to be on guard because there are forces against you that have a plan and if you fall into it, it could mean death for all that is important to you, both now and for eternity. You also have to be on guard against your flesh. The enemy will utilize your fleshly desires.

If the enemy can steal the word from you on your value, he can also take it for your marriage. If he can take it for your marriage, he will work hard to take it from you for your children. He will go into your career, your relationships, your finances, and everything that you hold dear. He will not quit until he has you and everyone connected to you dead.

That's how this works. So don't look at life and dwell on how hard it is. Don't look at your relationships and think of how difficult they are and how much they take from you. Realize that it will all seem hard, in the moment, until it isn't anymore because you've made it thru and past the issue. You have to grow. You have to be stretched. You a have to remember that anything worth having is worth fighting for.

Fight on your knees and as Nana says, don't live in the past.

If you ever feel that you need someone to pray for you, send me an email because that is one thing that I always do, pray.

My email address is makeda@makedarodriguez.com

Thank you for taking the time to read my book. I hope that you have found it a blessing and an encouragement for your life. I would love to hear from you and to know your thoughts regarding the topics that I have discussed. Send me an email and make sure to connect with me online.

About the Author

Makeda Rodriguez is a Christian woman living in the 21st century. She holds fundamental biblical principles dear to her heart. Not only are they dear to her heart, but they govern the way that she lives, acts, and loves. She is married to her high school sweetheart and they have four children. She is a devoted woman, wife, mother, friend, prayer warrior, author, coach, and entrepreneur. Although there is more that she loves about life, these are the most important. She is proud owner of a web design, development, virtual assistant, and digital solutions company called Red Word Host.

Along her journey of mothering, she has picked up a few hobbies and certifications, of those, her love of all things creative and planning. She has a Bachelor's degree in English and thoroughly enjoys reading. She has been trained as a Life Coach and is currently pursuing a masters in Adult and Higher Education.

She oversees Prayerful Bloggers an online ministry community for Christian women who blog. If you want to connect with her online, she can be found at http://beingmrsmom.com and on social media as @beingmrsmom She can be reached via email for at info@beingmrsmom.com

www.ingramcontent.com/pod-product-compliance
Lightning Source LLC
Chambersburg PA
CBHW071301110426
42743CB00042B/1134